BRITAIN IN TOMORROW'S WORLD

PRINCIPLES OF FOREIGN POLICY

CONTENTS

INTRODUCTION

'To play a leading part the English have got to know what they are doing. . . . The English will never develop into a nation of philosophers. They will always prefer instinct to logic . . . but they must get rid of their downright contempt for "cleverness".'

George Orwell[1]

BOOKS on British foreign policy usually fall into one of three categories. There are diplomatic histories which record and analyse the decisions of the past. There are treatises on diplomatic methods and there are books which criticize one type of policy or recommend another. This book has a different purpose. It is concerned with the theoretical concepts underlying the evolution and application of any British foreign policy: past, present or future; actual or potential. It does not suggest that any single theory exists, or could be conceived, capable of explaining the causes of past events or predicting the results of future decisions. Diplomacy is an art, not a science. The phenomena with which it is concerned are never precisely repeated and its motive forces are of uncertain direction, strength and duration. British foreign policy cannot be formulated in a general theory, not even in a 'General Theory of Relativity'.

Its practitioners are nevertheless compelled to employ, as the everyday tools of their work, certain theoretical assumptions, concepts and principles. It is the purpose of this book to identify these, to discuss their validity and utility, and to attempt their definition and classification.

[1] George Orwell, *The English People* (Collins 1947).

The result cannot be expected to resemble in any way the majestic and compelling formulations of the physical sciences. At best it may be possible to demonstrate that, when confronted by a practical problem, it is useful to ask certain theoretically based questions and, before choosing one of the alternative courses of action available, to apply certain theoretically indicated tests. This is a procedure familiar to doctors, whose training enables them to diagnose a disease from symptoms of which the cause is uncertain and to treat it by methods of proved efficacity but unexplained operation. Many theoretical arguments can be applied in practice long before they can be proved or accommodated within a satisfactorily unified system of thought.

The need for such theoretical arguments, indeed, the very possibility of their existence, would probably be disputed by most British politicians, diplomats and others concerned with foreign affairs. The British – especially, perhaps, the English – pride themselves on being pragmatists. They profess a horror of abstractions and systems. They decide every question on its merits in the light of common sense, experience and strictly factual knowledge. Most of those who shape or apply British foreign policy would indignantly deny that their decisions were, or should be, or even could be, reached on the basis of preconceived theories.

This is naturally nonsense. Every decision taken in the field of foreign policy is in fact influenced by purely theoretical considerations. The trouble is that these theories are seldom consciously held or systematically applied. All too often they have been acquired at second-hand, are out of date, imperfectly understood and of essentially sentimental origin. They tend to be formulated as slogans and are frequently described as 'my experience'. Many of them have, indeed, been evolved through the elevation to the status of a general principle of some conclusion drawn from a particular experience.

Lord Avon, for instance, explains in his Memoirs how

his experience of British foreign policy in the thirties convinced him that appeasement of Hitler and Mussolini had failed to prevent war from inflicting great loss and suffering on the people of Britain. He was thus basing himself on actual experience when he advanced, by analogy, the proposition that 'it would be as ineffective to show weakness to Nasser now (in 1956) in order to placate him as it was to show weakness to Mussolini'. But, when he went on to argue that 'the world would have suffered less if Hitler had been resisted on the Rhine, in Austria or in Czechoslovakia', he was putting forward a pure hypothesis about the supposed outcome of a course of action never actually adopted and of which neither he nor anyone else possessed any experience. Yet it was this hypothesis – elevated to an axiom and transferred to the Middle Eastern situation of 1956 – that determined Lord Avon's course of action in the Suez crisis, as he himself has explained in *Full Circle*[1] (the origin of the preceding quotations) and as subsequent historians have confirmed from independent sources.

But it was not only Lord Avon who was prompted by preconceived theory at the time of Suez. Many of his critics and opponents based their arguments on concepts of an even more abstract character: nationalism, anticolonialism, the 'double standard', the sanctity of the Charter of the United Nations. Even those professional diplomats who merely contended that the course of action followed by Lord Avon was unlikely to prove beneficial to British interests cannot escape the charge of raising issues of an essentially theoretical character. How can 'British interests' be defined? By what criteria can it be determined that a particular course of events either benefits or impairs 'British interests'? What tests can be applied in choosing the measures most likely to have results judged beneficial to 'British interests'? These are among the most important questions to be examined in the present work.

[1] Anthony Eden, *Full Circle* (Cassell 1960).

Two possible replies ought, perhaps, first to be disposed of. The first is that those concerned know instinctively what is good for Britain and that their common sense, their experience and their resulting powers of judgement enable them to decide without formal ratiocination how this can best be achieved. This romantic view was eloquently stated by Sir Harold Nicolson in his admirable biography of Lord Curzon,[1] who: 'was the last of that unbroken line of Foreign Secretaries who had been born with the privileges of a territorial aristocracy and nurtured on the traditions of a governing class. Eton and Winchester, Christ Church and Balliol, Trinity and King's had moulded these calm, confident and unassuming men. They had always known each other; they had always understood each other; they had always, from generation to generation, handed down the same standards of personal conduct and of public duty. Liberal or Conservative, Radical or Unionist – whatever shades of difference might divide them on domestic problems – upon the main principles of Imperial and Foreign Affairs they felt alike; they thought alike; they acted alike.'

Sir Harold Nicolson himself regarded this golden age of instinctive comprehension of the immutable principles of British foreign policy as having come to an end in 1924, when the advent of the first Labour Government inaugurated an era of controversy. Nevertheless, the essence of his view was restated, though in a more contemporary idiom, in a book published as late as 1962.[2] Lord Strang, writing with all the authority of a former Permanent Under-Secretary of State for Foreign Affairs, argues in his interesting essay on 'The Formation and Control of Foreign Policy' that British foreign policy was often:

> 'a dominant or prevailing trend, established only in part, if at all, by premeditated and predetermined intention, and revealing itself

[1] Harold Nicolson, *Curzon: The Last Phase* (Constable 1937).
[2] Lord Strang, *The Diplomatic Career.*

> through the cumulative effect of a succession of individual acts of greater or lesser moment, each decided upon in the light of practical international possibilities as they manifested themselves at the relevant time and under the impulse of a traditional manner of behaviour characteristic of the government concerned.'

Lord Strang went on to explain – and it is important to recall that, while serving in the Foreign Office at various levels he worked for governments of differing political views before, during and after the Second World War – that these successive decisions were seldom preceded by 'long and elaborate disquisitions'.

> 'Between Minister and officials who work together, there comes into existence a large area of common ground which all can take for granted and which does not need to be explained or demonstrated. This is why to the academic mind accustomed to the disciplines of scholarship, the proceedings of public servants so often bear an appearance of superficiality.'

The need for common ground, however, is not in dispute. Assumptions too generally accepted to require demonstration are an indispensable basis for most decisions and no academic would expect the engineer to question the formulae his textbooks provide – until the bridge collapses or the girder fails to bear its calculated load. Then, if human error is excluded, theories must be re-examined and assumptions tested anew. If public servants seem superficial, it is because they fail to question their assumptions when these no longer result in successful decisions. The idea of ministers and officials reaching rapid agreement through a common ability intuitively to perceive the proper basis for every decision would indeed be attractive, if it could only be demonstrated that this process usually produced the practical results intended. This is not a proposition which need be argued here. On the contrary, it would be singularly inappropriate, at the very outset of a work devoted to the thesis that assumptions require analysis and definition before they can properly provide a basis for judgement, to pronounce upon the 'success' of post-war British policy. Instead it seems preferable to dispose of this pragmatic objection by posing a rhetorical question: are the decisions of British foreign secretaries since the Second World War so generally agreed to have produced the desired results as to leave no grounds for questioning the methods by which these decisions were reached?

There are others, however, who would admit that the theoretical basis of British foreign policy is questionable, but would deny that it could be improved by analysis and definition. To this school the assumptions, concepts and principles underlying British foreign policy are a direct reflection of the class interests of those who control and execute this policy and can only be altered by radical changes in the political structure of Britain and the social composition of the Diplomatic Service. This argument, involving as it does the whole philosophy of Marxism, can scarcely be disposed of in a single paragraph. Indeed, it will be necessary to examine certain aspects of it more closely in subsequent chapters. Its adherents will fasten eagerly on the affinities between the views of Sir Harold Nicolson and Lord Strang and will be unmoved by any consideration of the social backgrounds of Lord Strang (the son of a tenant farmer) or of the Foreign Secretary with whom he most easily established 'common ground' – Mr. Bevin. Indeed, it is accepted mythology among critics of this persuasion that Mr. Bevin, that most unpliable man, was the blind and helpless tool of the Machiavellian aristocrats of the Foreign Office, a theory that could scarcely have survived much personal acquaintance with either Mr. Bevin or his officials. Yet this is only a retort. The true answer is that, whoever controls British foreign policy and from whatever motives, it remains of interest to examine the assumptions through which that control is exercised. To suppose that one particular controlling group is only capable of formulating one particular set of assumptions is surely carrying determinism beyond the belief of any student of twentieth-century history. The fundamental weakness of this book is not that its objective is either unnecessary or futile, but that it demanded a greater philosophic capacity and a profounder scholarship in its author. It should have emanated from some university, preferably from a faculty devoted expressly to the study of international relations and to the instruction in these matters of politicians, diplomats and others directly or indirectly concerned. The fifties and sixties of this century have witnessed an encouraging growth in the number of such institutions and of the theoretical studies they have engendered. So far, however, the prevailing trend has been to seek fundamental theories of universal application. The result has often been a degree of abstraction daunting to harassed practitioners in search of precepts. It is with their more parochial needs in mind that the present work is humbly offered, not to fill, but to exploit, the gap now existing between 'What to Do About Vietnam' and 'A General Theory of International Relations'. If no such gap existed, if the theoretical basis of British foreign policy had ever been established with authority and conviction, this ramshackle skiff would never have been launched on such uncharted waters. It will not be the first time that, as Sir Harold Nicolson observed, 'the art of diplomacy, as that of water-colours, has suffered much from the fascination which it exercises upon the amateur'.[1] But the alternative to amateurism is not abstention and, if this book fails to provide an adequate theoretical guide to practitioners in the field of foreign affairs, it may at least enrage some academic into remedying its deficiencies.

[1] Harold Nicolson, op. cit.

I

WHAT IS FOREIGN POLICY?

'Some were so simple as to imagine that the department of State known as the Foreign Office was a tribunal for inflicting injustices upon aliens.'

Roger Grinstead[1]

A CHARACTERISTIC difficulty of this confused and complex subject is the absence of any generally accepted definition of the phrase 'foreign policy'. Sir Harold Nicolson, in all the years he devoted to urging the importance of distinguishing between foreign policy and diplomacy, was content to define the latter alone. Professor Carr's two great works *The Twenty Years Crisis* and *Conditions of Peace*, are major contributions to the theory of foreign policy, but he found it unnecessary to define his subject. So did Messrs. Woodward and Butler, the editors of the countless volumes of *Documents on British Foreign Policy* and so do nine out of every ten of those writers who incorporate in the title of their works the words 'British Foreign Policy'. There can be few other subjects where it is so generally taken for granted, even by scholars, that the reader will automatically understand its scope. As for the dictionaries and encyclopaedias – even such an avowedly specialized work as the *Penguin Dictionary of Politics* – they often ignore the very existence of the expression 'foreign policy'.

To deplore this reticence is more than pedantry. There are entities too generally comprehended to require definition, but foreign policy is not among them. Elec-

[1] Roger Grinstead, *Some Talk of Alexander* (Secker & Warburg 1943).

tricity, for instance, is daily manipulated by millions incapable of defining its nature. But electricity has two advantages denied to foreign policy: first, electricity is readily distinguishable from coal or a candle; second, electricity is known to inflict upon the entirely ignorant meddler a shock that is sometimes lethal and always painful. With foreign policy the suffering is humanity's.

Some English pragmatists will repudiate this distinction. Just as, for all practical purposes, electricity is a source of light, heat and power emanating from two holes in the wall, so foreign policy is the business of the Foreign Office. Indeed, this is clearly the criterion – perhaps the involuntary criterion – adopted by Messrs. Woodward and Butler in their compilation of *Documents on British Foreign Policy*. These innumerable volumes include precisely two documents (one of them the text of a press release) explaining the reasons for a decision which, of all those taken by a British Government between 1919 and 1939, was perhaps among the most potent, the most far-reaching and the most long-lasting in its influence upon international affairs: the decision, on 20 September 1931, to abandon the Gold Standard.[1]

No blame whatever attaches to these distinguished editors. Although, as historians, they were undoubtedly aware of the significance of this event and although, in the words of the Preface to Volume II of the Second Series of this collection, they were 'given unreserved access to the whole of the Foreign Office archives', it is highly unlikely that these contained additional material of any significance. In 1931 the management of the British economy and the parity of the pound sterling were regarded as altogether outside the competence of the Foreign Office. Both were held to be the subject of immutable laws of a nature that was partly moral, partly scientific and wholly mystic. It is improbable that the opinions of the Foreign Office on the

[1] E. L. Woodward & Rohan Butler, *Documents on British Policy 1919–1939*; Second Series, Volume II, Chapter IV (H.M.S.O. 1947).

international repercussions of decisions in this sphere would even have been sought, still less heeded. Yet in what sense can it be contended that leaving the Gold Standard was less of a foreign policy decision than the signature of the Treaty of Locarno, a step regarded at the time as possessing the utmost significance, but which ultimately left singularly little trace of its influence on the history of the period?

Future delvers in the archives, however, are likely to find a larger and more variegated selection of documents for the fifties and sixties. From 1961 to 1963, for instance, newspaper readers discovered with awe the almost limitless range of expertise demanded of Mr. Heath and the members of the Foreign Office who seconded his efforts to negotiate British entry to the European Economic Community. From the harmonization of social insurance for migrant workers to the single market for pigmeat there seemed to be no aspect of governmental activity beyond their purview, except perhaps those once typical manifestations of foreign policy: 'peace, war, neutrality and alliance or various combinations of or approaches to these.'[1] Nor can Foreign Office involvement in all these matters be dismissed as the mere exercise of diplomacy – the negotiation of a policy devised by others. Mr. Heath throughout made clear that he was as much a composer as an executant.

The Foreign Office were not, however, the only department engaged in the elaboration and modification of British policy towards the Common Market. Not only did Mr. Heath's advisers include representatives of other Ministries, but the participation of Home Departments in international negotiations and in the devising of British policy on international issues is standard practice. In July 1968, for instance, seventeen Public Departments in addition to the Foreign Office and those vanishing symbols of an older era, the Commonwealth and Colonial Offices, were listed as possessing at least one section devoted to

[1] Webster's *Third New International Dictionary*.

international affairs.[1] Many of these also had their own representatives attached to Embassies abroad and their very designations – 'Counsellor (Development)', 'First Secretary (Civil Air)', 'Scientific Attaché' – would have bewildered Sir Edward Grey or his officials.

Indeed, the most elementary research is enough to reveal a degree of overlapping, even of paradox, that makes it impossible to define foreign policy as the business of the Foreign Office or even, more broadly, as those aspects of Government policy which mainly concern foreigners. The Home Office, for instance, employ a large staff to decide which foreigners shall be admitted to Britain, how they shall be treated on arrival, how long and on what conditions they may remain and with what degree of ignominy they shall be expelled. So many foreigners visit the British Isles every year that it would scarcely be too hazardous a guess to suppose that the Home Office sharply influence the destiny of more individual foreigners than ever become conscious of the existence of the British Foreign Office. Nor is this a simple matter of domestic administration. Whether in such minor incidents as the stripping of Miss Eriksson at Gatwick Airport on 17 March 1967 or in the crescendo of international protest that has followed successive Immigration Acts, the policy of the Home Office constantly affects Britain's reputation abroad and her relations with other countries. Yet, when it comes to the liberty of British subjects and their right to travel, it is the Foreign Secretary who grants, refuses or withdraws their passports.

As so often when the English are illogical, there is some reason behind this apparent confusion of functions. In the modern world the range of governmental decisions without repercussion beyond the shores of Britain is shrinking

[1] Her Majesty's Ministers and Heads of Public Departments', H.M.S.O. Even this cannot be a complete list of British agencies engaged in international relations: it does not, for instance, include the Bank of England.

daily. Foot and mouth disease, unemployment insurance and the inspection of nuclear power stations have all become subjects for international discussion and negotiation. Eventually every public department or governmental agency may have its international section and its overseas representatives. What functions will then remain for the Foreign Office and in what sense can it be argued that *foreign policy*, even now, constitutes a single and distinct branch of governmental policy?

As Mr. A. J. P. Taylor has pointed out in his interesting book *The Trouble Makers*[1], there has long been a school of thought which contends that foreign policy is a needless evil. Mr. Taylor, for instance, quotes Cobden as advocating 'as little intercourse as possible between governments; as much connexion as possible between the nations of the world' and says that his favourite toast was 'no foreign politics'. Might not a modern Cobdenite argue that the beneficent tasks of the Foreign Office – reaching agreement on practical issues – should be split up among the international sections of the functional Home Departments and that the residue – 'typically manifested in peace, war, neutrality and alliance' – could safely be allowed to wither away in a country whose diminished power and pretensions would never require such sinister activities if they were not artificially fostered by a Department possessing no other *raison d'être*?

Theoretically this question is not quite as absurd as it sounds. Given that all systems of government entail a series of vertical hierarchies, each devoted to a particular branch of activity, and that these vertical structures must be intersected by systems of horizontal co-ordination, there are many ways in which this could conceivably be arranged. At present, for instance, it is arguable that British relations with the United States, being conducted through such multifarious channels and involving so many issues comprehensible only to a handful of experts, have already

[1] A. J. P. Taylor, *The Trouble Makers* (Hamish Hamilton 1957).

expanded beyond the control of the Foreign Office. Could anyone – even the Head of the Foreign Office – furnish a complete list of all the issues under discussion at any given moment between British and American governmental agencies?

Nor, as a glance at the Diplomatic Service List will reveal, is Washington the only capital where diplomats are outnumbered by the representatives of other British Government Departments or Agencies, each pursuing his particular line of business at the behest of his own superiors at home. Is it perhaps the ultimate destiny of Ambassadors to relegate to a handful of diplomatic attachés their traditional functions and themselves to become the overseas equivalents of the war-time Regional Commissioners? Would there then still be a distinct and separate foreign policy for such an Ambassador to implement or would his tasks be confined to co-ordination and representation? Would there still be a Foreign Office or simply a collection of co-ordinating committees in Whitehall? The American Committee, for instance, might meet periodically to resolve any conflict between the instructions of, say, the Ministry of Technology and the Ministry of Power, which the Ambassador (the usual arbiter) had exceptionally been unable to settle in Washington.

In the world of the future it is not inconceivable that this Cobdenite vision, which still has its supporters, may actually come to pass. For the moment, however, it would not meet the requirements of the system of nation-states we know today. Human beings, whether individually or collectively, are constantly confronted by conflict in their respective interests and aspirations. Not all these conflicts are, or even can be, resolved by a mutually acceptable compromise. Within the nation-state there is usually some superior authority able to persuade, to order or even to coerce the parties into acceptance of a solution. Beyond its borders no such authority exists. If a British agency cannot reach agreement with an American agency, there is seldom any third party capable of resolving the dispute. One or other must give way or else attempt coercion. Of course a similar situation can arise within the nation-state: a trade union may attempt to coerce an employer. But the structure of the nation-state, and its laws, are generally such as to set limits to this coercion, thus ensuring that one side or the other gives way before intolerable damage is inflicted on the community at large. Imperfectly as these arrangements operate in practice, there is, in Britain at least, sufficient acceptance of a general national interest transcending the interests of individuals or groups for it to be possible to permit considerable latitude in the pursuit of sectional interests. The public as a whole may be inconvenienced; it may even suffer financial loss: it will not normally be assaulted, starved or even terrorized.

No similar restraints govern the evolution of disputes with another nation-state. When a conflict of interests arose, for instance, between British and Icelandic fishermen, violence quickly developed, warships intervened on both sides and agreement was ultimately reached only because both governments came to agree that more important issues were involved than the interests or aspirations of their respective fishermen. This was not, incidentally, a controversy which offered much support either to the arguments of Mr. Cobden or to that later proposition of Lord Russell:

> 'The interests of the British democracy do not conflict at any point with the interests of mankind. The interests of the British governing classes conflict at many points . . .'[1]

Here it was the interests of the democracy that provoked the conflict and those of the governing classes that eventually resolved it.

Within Britain, therefore, the consequences to the community of a dispute between two of its sections are limited by the superior authority of the State. But, once a

[1] Lord Russell, *Foreign Policy of the Entente*. Quoted in Taylor, op. cit.

British subject, a section of the British people, or a British private or official organization becomes involved in a dispute with foreigners, the traditional rules no longer apply. There are no limits to the possible repercussions on the British people as a whole. In the absence, therefore, of any international authority capable of effective action in such matters, it becomes necessary for the British Government to maintain relations with foreign governments with a view to the prevention, limitation or determination of disputes between British subjects and foreigners. The conduct of these relations has to be centralized because, even if the British Government were to regard a particular conflict as a private matter, it does not follow that the foreign government will adopt a similar attitude and, once British subjects or a British organization discover that their private quarrel has attracted the hostile intervention of a foreign government, they will demand support from their own. This may, or may not, be forthcoming, but it is clearly impossible to leave the decision – whether to defend a British fishing-boat arrested by an Icelandic frigate – to the sole discretion of the nearest British naval officer. Whatever he decides, and whatever the practical outcome of that decision, there will be repercussions which it is not within the sole power of the British Government to limit.

British foreign policy, therefore, is essentially concerned with disputes between British subjects, British organizations and British governmental agencies, on the one hand, and those of foreign States on the other. If there were no likelihood of such disputes arising, or if there existed an international authority capable of enforcing acceptable decisions, or if the British people were invariably content to accept the judgement of the foreign government concerned, there would be no need for Britain to maintain foreign relations or for the British Government to devise a policy for their conduct. None of these conditions is likely to be fulfilled in the foreseeable future.

To maintain that the central direction of British relations with foreign governments, and hence the need for the existence as a separate entity of foreign policy, arises solely from the possibility of disagreement, may seem a depressingly negative view. Should not the emphasis be more positive: on the possibilities of international co-operation and of a common striving for the amelioration of the human race? These are fine phrases, but a moment's reflection, and a few practical examples, should confirm this seemingly cynical conclusion and assist the search for a definition of the term 'foreign policy'.

British subjects contemplating a pleasant holiday in the South of France seldom consult the Foreign Office in advance or register on arrival with the nearest British consul. These are precautions taken when trouble is expected. If the competent British and French ministers are in entire agreement about the joint construction of a new aircraft, they will at most ascertain from their respective foreign offices that such co-operation is unlikely to create difficulties elsewhere. It is only when disputes arise that the diplomats are involved. If all the Ministers of Health of the entire world were to meet in conference and agree upon measures for the eradication of malaria, they might call upon their diplomats to draft or to interpret, but no question of foreign policy would arise in the absence of dispute.

In a sense Cobden was right: if connexions between the peoples of the world were invariably amical, there would be no need of foreign politics and we should all be better off. It is this consideration which often prompts the expert in other fields – the scientist, the doctor or the engineer – to echo Cobden and blame all human conflict on the pernicious activities of politicians and diplomats. The British physicist experiences no difficulty in convincing his Russian colleague of the truth of his latest equation; he receives generous hospitality; he discovers common tastes and he exchanges a number of uplifting platitudes. If there are obstacles to complete Anglo-Russian friendship these can, he concludes, only come from the diplomats. His sentiments are echoed by everyone who has successfully established the existence of a particular interest uniting individual nationals, or even government agencies, of two States whose general policies are nevertheless conflicting. Leave it to us practical men, is the cry, to reach agreement on practical matters. Why drag politics into it?

A preliminary answer to this question may be found in one of the most elegant and enthralling of modern British historical works, Mr. Trevor-Roper's *The Last Days of Hitler*.[1] Writing of Hitler's exceptionally able Minister of Armaments, an architect by profession, Trevor-Roper says:

> 'Speer was a technocrat and nourished a technocrat's philosophy. To the technocrat, as to the Marxist, politics are irrelevant. To him the prosperity, the future of a people depends not upon the personalities who happen to hold political office, nor upon the institutions in which their relations are formalized – these are irrelevant phenomena of no ultimate significance – but upon the technical instruments whereby society is maintained, on the roads and railways, the canals and bridges, the services and factories wherein a nation invests its labour, and whence it draws its wealth. This is a very convenient philosophy; and it is true that in certain times (so long, that is, as they can be taken for granted) politics can be ignored. For nearly two years after he had succeeded Todt as Armaments Minister, Speer found that he could take politics for granted, merely observing the antics of the politicians from his favoured seat in the royal box, while he concentrated his activities and interests upon the communications and factories which he so completely understood. Then he was disillusioned. When Hitler and Goebbels raised the slogan of "Scorched Earth", and called upon the German people to destroy their towns and factories, to sacrifice their railways and rolling-stock for the sake of a myth and a Wagnerian Twilight, then at last the fallacy of his philosophy became apparent to Speer. Politics do matter; politicians can effect the destiny of nations.'

[1] H. R. Trevor-Roper, *The Last Days of Hitler* (MacMillan 1950).

All these digressions, all this casting to and fro for arguments to refute objections (even if they will have to be considered again in later chapters) have nevertheless narrowed the search for a definition. The subject-matter of British foreign policy is not restricted to the functions at any given time of the Foreign Office; yet it need not include all British relations with foreigners or foreign governments: foreign policy is concerned with disagreement, or the possibility of disagreement, with foreign governments.

At first sight, this limitation of the subject-matter of foreign policy to issues involving actual or potential dispute with foreign governments scarcely seems to constitute much of an advance. History suggests that nothing is too trivial or too remote to provide the grounds for dispute among nation-states. Nevertheless, even if the raw material of foreign policy remains unlimited (as witness the signature in 1967 of a Treaty on Principles Governing the Activities of States in the Exploration and Use of Outer Space including the Moon and Other Celestial Bodies) the character of foreign policy itself can be more closely defined by introducing as its *raison d'être* the possibility of disagreement. The British Government, for instance, maintain a Ministry of Labour and a 'labour policy'. 'Labour' is a term applicable to most human activities (even the composition of this book), but neither the Ministry nor the policy of the Government are much concerned with those aspects of labour involving no risk of disagreement. Their purpose is primarily to identify causes of dispute and, if disputes cannot be prevented, to resolve them or limit their consequences. Only the most extreme devotees of the classical doctrines of political economy would nowadays regard the existence of a Department of State with such objectives as either unnecessary or undesirable and, though the Cobdenite arguments will be further discussed in later chapters, this analogy may perhaps be offered as a provisional justification for the existence of foreign policy as well.

Foreign policy, then, is not necessarily, or even primarily, manifested 'in peace, war, neutrality and alliance', nor is it restricted to those subjects which tradition, chance or inertia may, at any given moment, induce the British Government to regard as the proper concern of the Foreign Office. Instead, foreign policy may now be defined as: 'that general conception of national aspirations, interests and capacities which influences the Government in the identification of disputes with other governments and in the choice of methods for the prevention, determination or limitation of such disputes.'

The several components of this definition will be examined at length in subsequent chapters. But, as this formula is to provide the central core of the entire book, it may meanwhile be desirable to explain briefly why this form of words has been chosen and to provide at least a prima facie case for its further consideration.

Taking the definition phrase by phrase, foreign policy is described as a '*general conception*' to distinguish it from the kind of *ad hoc* assessment that may precede a particular decision. For instance, when President Nasser announced the nationalization of the Suez Canal in 1956, the identification of this step as entailing Anglo-Egyptian disagreement, together with an appreciation of its likely repercussions on British interests and of the capacities available to the British Government for limiting or terminating this dispute, would undoubtedly have been the subject of assessments specially prepared by the Foreign Office and other Departments concerned. Such assessments might not, however, have covered 'national aspirations' for, as Lord Strang remarked with a touch of unwonted acid, 'it is supposed to be the politician's particular business' to identify and interpret 'the general sentiment of the public'.[1] Nevertheless, as was earlier established from Lord Avon's Memoirs, the decisive influence on the eventual decision was a general conception

[1] Op. cit.

much wider in scope than anything directly arising from the Suez Canal.

'*National aspirations*' is a more difficult term to define or to distinguish from '*national interests*', but it is employed to mean what the British people want as opposed to what they need. The acutely controversial process of discriminating between these two concepts will be the theme of subsequent chapters, but the following instance may serve to appease the indignant reader meanwhile: it is arguable that the British people want slavery to be abolished in Saudi Arabia, whereas they need to import Saudi Arabian oil. The first would thus be an 'aspiration'; the second an 'interest'. '*National capacities*', on the other hand, are the resources available to the Government for the furtherance of their objectives.

The rôle of foreign policy in the '*identification of disputes*' is perhaps more obvious. Every day hundreds of telegrams pour into the Foreign Office reporting events all over the world; a *coup d'état* has been launched in Greece; an Egyptian battery has fired on an Israeli vessel in the Gulf of Akaba; the Government of Iraq has prohibited the export of oil. To determine which of these events might involve the British Government in disagreement with a foreign government it is not enough to possess a comprehensive knowledge of the facts of each case: there must also be some general conception of the British interests on which these events may impinge.

The '*prevention*' of disputes scarcely requires any immediate explanation, but '*determination*' is intended to mean putting an end to the dispute, whereas '*limitation*' implies action to restrict the number of parties to the dispute, or the scope of the dispute or the repercussions of the dispute.

Analysis of the implications of this general definition and of its component parts will determine the shape and structure of this book. But the purpose, and this must be emphasized yet again, will not be to formulate an actual

British foreign policy, to set it down on one side of a sheet of paper. This would be a fruitless task. The range of subjects to be covered is too vast; the factors which must influence decisions are too variable; the process of change in the aspirations, the interests and, above all, the capacities of the British people is too rapid and unremitting. Any such formulation must either cover every foreseeable contingency, in which case it would be out of date before it was ever finished; or else state abstract principles in terms too general to constitute a useful guide to practical decisions.

Curiously enough, Lord Strang (in most of his published works a forceful advocate of the pragmatic approach to foreign affairs and an effective critic of the limited value of theoretical studies) has himself provided a striking example of the abstract definition and its weaknesses. In 1951, so he explains in *Home and Abroad*,[1] Lord Strang was asked by Mr. Bevin 'to write down for him on one sheet of paper the main objectives of the foreign policy which he had been trying to conduct. This is what I wrote:

> 'During the past five years, the objects of British policy have been:
>
> First, to defend British interests and cherish the good name of the United Kingdom.
>
> Secondly, to help to build up the strength and cohesion and prosperity of the free world in the spirit of the Charter of the United Nations on the triple basis of intimate co-operation with the United States of America, with the other members of the Commonwealth family and with the nations of Western Europe, by the conclusion of constructive agreements like those for Western Union, the European Recovery Programme and the North Atlantic Treaty.
>
> Thirdly, to promote the well-being of the peoples of the Middle East and to work for the security of that area, the key to

[1] Lord Strang, *House and Abroad* (André Deutsch 1956).

which would be an understanding freely negotiated on equal terms with Egypt.

Fourthly, to maintain and develop a beneficent and fruitful partnership between the Western peoples and the peoples of South and South-East Asia in the critical period of their assumption of independent nationhood. Of that partnership, the Colombo Plan is a type.

Finally, to neglect no fair opportunity to seek by patient negotiation and mutual accord to relax international tensions wherever they may be, and to free the minds of men and women from the haunting fear of war so that they and their children may live their industrious lives in security and peace.'

These are fine sentiments which would embellish any public speech by a British Foreign Secretary or Ambassador, but which could not readily be employed as conclusive arguments with which to support a recommendation for specific action. It is not on the basis of such sentiments that practical decisions are taken.

And the purpose of this book is to facilitate practical decisions by reducing to the simplest and most generally valid terms those theoretical criteria which ought, so it is contended, to form the tacit foundation for every detailed assessment of the particular problems confronting those charged with the shaping and execution of British foreign policy.

2

NATIONAL ASPIRATIONS

'I shall continue to do what is right, whether you like it or not, whether the country likes it or not.'

Mr. Selwyn Lloyd when Foreign Secretary[1]

'The Communist Party was, is and will be the only ruler of thoughts, the mouthpiece of ideas and aspirations.'

PRAVDA[2]

IN considering national aspirations as an element in the evolution of foreign policy, three questions must first be answered: what makes an aspiration 'national'; what distinguishes it from an 'interest'; what makes it relevant to foreign policy? If satisfactory answers can be found to these essentially theoretical questions, it should then be possible to pose a further question of a more practical character: how do those concerned with the shaping and execution of foreign policy identify the particular national aspirations which they ought to take into account?

The answer to the first question must be disappointingly empirical. An 'aspiration' becomes 'national' when it is so regarded by the government of the day. British constitutional practice does not provide for referenda or plebiscites; general elections, though often concerned with foreign affairs are never solely so concerned; public opinion polls, whatever may be thought of the validity of their minute samples in providing answers to such simple questions as 'Will you vote Labour or Conservative?', are

[1] A speech to his constituents, *The Times*, 30 March 1957.

[2] *Pravda*, 6 July 1956.

unsuited to eliciting clear answers on the more complex issues of foreign policy. It is thus seldom possible to support by convincing evidence any assertion that the majority of the British people share some meaningful aspiration relevant to foreign policy.

A few recent examples, beginning with the most obvious exception, may help to support this proposition. This exception was the so-called 'Peace Ballot' of 1935. This asked five specific questions, beginning with,

> Should Great Britain remain a member of the League of Nations?

and ending with,

> Do you consider that if a nation insists on attacking another, the other nations should combine to compel it to stop by:
> (*a*) economic and non-military measures?
> (*b*) if necessary military measures?

According to Sir Anthony Eden[1] 10 million people said 'yes' to 'economic and non-military measures', whereas 6,784,000 said 'yes' to military measures, and 2,351,000 said 'no'. As some 20 million people voted in the General Election later that year, this ballot provided the British Government of the day with exceptionally strong and up-to-date evidence of national aspirations bearing on a topical international issue – Italian aggression against Abyssinia. It appears to have exercised correspondingly great influence on the government of the day, who did indeed invoke the machinery of the League of Nations against Italy and resort to economic and non-military measures. Their decision to abstain from military measures, or from economic measures likely to lead to war, seems to have been based primarily on a different assessment of national interests and capacities, though some writers have argued either that Ministers failed to appreciate the significance of the majority in favour of military measures

[1] *Facing the Dictators*, Chapter XIII (Cassell 1962).

or else considered that this majority did not understand the full implications of their view.

On no other international issue of the last fifty years has there been such a convincingly clear-cut demonstration that a majority of the British people shared a particular national aspiration. Even the national will to victory manifested in such practical form during the Second World War scarcely constitutes an exception, for this did not become overwhelmingly evident until the only remaining alternative was surrender to German rule. If the British guarantee to Poland or even the ultimatum to Germany of 3 September 1939, had first been made the subject of a national plebiscite, there might not have been much of a majority in favour of either course.

Certainly on other occasions when British public opinion, or that section of it concerned with such matters, was excited by international issues, there was generally a substantial measure of disagreement. For instance, from 1919 to 1923 those who cried 'make Germany pay for the war' were answered by the advocates of reconciliation, while the desire to combat 'the foul baboonery' of Bolshevism clashed with the slogan 'Hands off Russia'. Constitutional advance in India, the Japanese invasion of Manchuria, the later stages of the Abyssinia crisis, the Spanish Civil War and successive German acts of aggression all revealed the existence of conflicting aspirations among at least sections of the British people. In more recent years the Suez Affair of 1956 divided the politically interested with a bitterness unequalled since the Munich Crisis of 1938 and, later still, those urging the Government to dissociate Britain from American 'aggression' in Vietnam were answered by those who would support American defence of this corner of the 'Free World' with British troops.

These are by no means the only occasions when sections of the British people have expressed – by attendance at public meetings, by letters and telegrams to Ministers and

Members of Parliament, by marches and demonstrations and, though this is often hard to interpret, by voting in by-elections – their support for sharply divergent views. Except, perhaps, for brief periods during the Second World War, no politician has ever been able to assert uncontradicted that one particular opinion represented the unanimous wish of the people.

How, then, is the politician genuinely concerned to give effect to the aspirations of the people to judge which of the opinions advanced by different groups most nearly represents the national will? The methods of physical science are not applicable: the force and direction of opinions cannot be measured, nor can their interaction be so calculated as to express the resultant of many diverse views in a single tendency. The indicators on which the politician relies are at best straws in the wind: he can only try to divine the wishes of the usually silent and indifferent majority from the expressed views of the small groups able and willing to manifest their opinions. Some politicians claim a high degree of success: Lord Baldwin was fond of saying that his worst enemy could not claim that he did not understand the people of England.[1] Yet, in the absence of objective tests, the constant inability of politicians to reach agreement in their assessment of popular wishes can only induce the detached observer to regard with considerable scepticism any assertion of the existence of specifically 'national' aspirations in the field of foreign affairs.

Politicians, however, cannot afford such philosophic doubts. They are elected to represent the people and to give effect to the wishes of the people. If these wishes cannot be ascertained with precision and certainty, it becomes the duty of the politician to guess, and guess he does. Sometimes his guesswork may be coloured because, consciously or unconsciously, he attaches added weight to the views of his supporters or to views which coincide with his

[1] G. M. Young, *Stanley Baldwin* (Rupert Hart-Davis 1952).

own. Occasionally he will assert the existence of a national aspiration merely to strengthen the case for a course of action decided on other grounds. However he arrives at his assessment, its accuracy will often prove just as difficult to refute as it is to establish. Moreover, when politicians form a government and are thus able to make of their assessment of popular wishes an effective influence on the shaping and execution of policy, they can often create a firmer basis for their guesswork. There is a strong nationalist, even chauvinist, streak in the British people and any given stance in foreign affairs will often command greater public support once it has actually been adopted by a British Government than it did when it was merely proposed by a political party. If Ministers take a decision and that decision is opposed by foreigners, it will sometimes be possible for the British Government to produce sufficient evidence of popular support to claim as a national aspiration a policy never previously suggested to the electorate. Politicians are the moulders, as well as the mouthpieces, of public opinion and no one has greater opportunities to foster, to suppress, or even to create, a national aspiration than the Government of the day. However unsatisfactory this may seem to the philosopher and whatever the verdict of the historian on the actual results, there is no practical alternative to initial reliance on the judgement of the British Government as a guide to identifying particular opinions as the 'national' aspirations of the British people.

This is naturally not an infallible indicator. Governments have taken decisions which subsequently attracted sufficient opposition to compel a reversal of policy: the Hoare–Laval agreement of 1935 had to be abandoned and the Foreign Secretary's resignation accepted because of adverse reactions in Parliament and outside. The judgement of Ministers provides an imperfect test, but it is the one commonly applied in practice.

If the 'national' character of an aspiration is so nebulous, so uncertain and so dependent on the subjective judgement of a handful of Ministers, how are we to differentiate an 'aspiration' from an 'interest'? In theory, at least, this is less of a problem. When the supporters of a particular course of action advance as their main arguments considerations of an ethical or sentimental character – justice, honour, obligation, gratitude, the principles of democracy, the interests of humanity, the natural instincts of repugnance or esteem – they are expressing an aspiration. When they invoke the likelihood of early and material advantage to the British people, they are expressing an interest. In practice, unfortunately, both kinds of argument are commonly employed. Those advocating British intervention in the internal affairs of Rhodesia, for instance, did not rely only on ethical considerations, but also contended that such intervention would help to avert a widespread racial conflict potentially injurious to the material interests of the British people. Their opponents appealed to the sentiments of the British people towards their 'kith and kin' to reinforce the statistics of lost British trade. Yet, without trespassing too far on the subject matter of the following chapter, it may provisionally be reasonable to suggest a practical test. The more plausibly the predicted results of a given course of action can be expressed in quantitative terms of material advantage or disadvantage to be sustained by the British people at a definite future date, the more likely it is that the argument is based on interest. If the consequences cannot be predicted with any degree of confidence, or if their effects on the British people can only be expressed in abstract terms or if the predicted date for these effects is either remote or altogether uncertain or if the British people are only to share in advantages or disadvantages to be incurred by the entire human race, it becomes increasingly difficult to regard the national interest as significantly involved. To put it in simpler and more arbitrary terms, a government endeavouring to satisfy national aspirations is concerned with the emotional needs of the people; a government considering national interests with their more material necessities.

Naturally it does not follow that any necessary conflict exists between national aspirations and national interests. Similar conclusions may be reached by more than one process of reasoning from different premises. It may even be argued that this distinction between interest and aspiration, though conceivably valid for particular cases, loses its significance when applied to the broader and more enduring concepts so far ignored in this chapter. Are not peace, security, independence, the freedom of the seas and a variety of other principles daily enunciated by British politicians as firmly grounded on interest as on aspiration? Why quibble about the extent of popular support for sanctions against Italy – or Rhodesia – when we can be sure that the British people want peace, international justice and racial toleration?

The answer to these objections lies in our third test of national aspirations: that of relevance. An aspiration is relevant to foreign policy when it suggests to the Government which of the various courses reasonably open to it in foreign policy most nearly corresponds to popular wishes. As foreign policy is primarily concerned with disputes, this means that national aspirations should help the Government to decide which issues the people consider worth disputing, how those disputes should be conducted and, in the last resort, what criteria should determine the choice between giving way and using force. Merely to say that the British people want peace – an assertion which no British Foreign Secretary and hardly anyone else in Britain would deny – offers no assistance in this process. The crucial question is one of relative priorities: which other aspirations are the British people willing to sacrifice for the preservation of peace and in what circumstances?

This is far from being an academic question or even an extreme and exceptional case. Since 1945 every British Government has constantly been involved in disputes demanding a choice between giving way and resorting to force. Some of these choices could have led to war on a scale capable of jeopardizing the continued existence of the British people: the decision to defy the Russian blockade of West Berlin or to join in the defence of South Korea. Others have merely sent British soldiers, sailors and airmen to their deaths in places and causes now only dimly remembered: Palestine, Indonesia, the Corfu Straits, Malaya, China, Kenya, Cyprus, Egypt, Malaysia, British Guiana, Kuwait, Aden. Not a year has passed since 1945 without British forces going into action somewhere in the world, sometimes in circumstances that could have led to more than the handful of deaths so easily overlooked by those preoccupied with the nightmare of nuclear Armageddon.[1] And, for every dispute in which the British Government have decided to fight, there have been half a dozen in which they have submitted to foreign violence of a character that might once have led to war: the destruction of British embassies, ships, aircraft and property abroad; murder, kidnapping and outrage of British subjects; armed aggression against British allies and dependencies.

Amid the passions, the anarchy and the violence of the twentieth century, there is no question on which the British Government have a greater need to know the wishes of their people than this: when to yield and when to fight.

This is not an impossible question to answer even in the simplified and general terms likely to command widespread popular understanding and support. If the slogan 'better red than dead' were ever to be generally accepted, this could constitute a valid national aspiration. It would clearly indicate to the British Government that no dispute with the Soviet Government should ever be pursued to the point of war and that in no circumstances should a Soviet

[1] 'British forces have not been in action anywhere in the world. No one has been killed or wounded in action anywhere in the world in the last 12 months – the first time this has happened in this century.' – Mr Reynolds, Minister of Defence for Administration, reported in *The Times*, 6 March 1969.

ultimatum be rejected. 'Make love, not war', on the other hand, is irrelevant: it cannot apply to governments, only to individuals, and, when literally implemented by a British politician, its results were by no means those intended. As for the great abstractions – peace, honour, justice, humanity – their employment, whether singly or in combination, produces only noise: sound without sense. Anyone tempted to chant them in Downing Street would do better to substitute the word 'rhubarb', now widely used to symbolize mass emotion.

Even more elaborate and sophisticated formulations can still fail the basic test of relevancy – and therefore of utility – unless they provide clear guidance on what to yield and when to fight. In 1935, for instance, Lord Attlee, then leader of the opposition, urged the Government to 'make support of the League (of Nations) the whole basis of its policy. I emphasize the point, the whole basis of its policy.'[1] Today someone might express similar views by urging the Government to submit to the judgement of the United Nations all disputes incapable of resolution by negotiation. Even if those concerned were willing to accept an adverse verdict from the United Nations – to hand over the people of Gibraltar to Spain today or perhaps those of the Channel Islands to France tomorrow – such an aspiration would still lack relevance because it frequently happens that the United Nations are unable either to agree on a judgement or to enforce it. Anyone wishing to assert as a national aspiration the submission of all disputes to the United Nations would have to go further. He might say:

'When the British Government are unable to resolve a dispute by negotiation, this should be submitted to the United Nations and, if the United Nations fail to terminate the dispute, the British Government should give way to the other party concerned rather than consider any other means of resolving the dispute.'

[1] Lord Attlee, *As It Happened*, Chapter XII (Heinemann 1954).

Or he might so qualify his original proposition as to specify exceptions or to provide for alternative courses of action. But it is inadequate to urge the British Government to choose a particular course of action without regard to the different choices open to other governments. The mother who tells her young son not to quarrel with other boys must expect the question: 'but what shall I do if they quarrel with me?' She may advise turning the other cheek or a punch on the nose, but to answer 'if you don't quarrel with them, they won't quarrel with you' would be to display sufficient ignorance of the real world to forfeit her son's respect for maternal advice. To be relevant to foreign policy a national aspiration must envisage the possible existence of foreign opposition, and offer some guidance to the British Government in their choice of methods for meeting this opposition.

The practising politician may regard such a condition, indeed, the whole of this argument, as hopelessly academic. He might concede that foreign policy is about disputes, that disputes often lead to conflict and that the British Government should know roughly how far the British people are prepared to go either in yielding in order to preserve peace or in risking war in order to promote other objectives. But the idea of demanding from the British people the expression of their aspirations in terms so rigidly consistent and consequential would seem to him neither possible nor necessary. In real life, he would argue, people do not think, but feel, and politicians instinctively interpret popular sentiments without these having to be formulated in language better adapted to the study than the parish hall.

This is a compelling, but also a convenient argument. The more vaguely and loosely popular sentiments are expressed, the greater the freedom of the politician, not only to choose his course of action as he wishes, but also, if need be, to excuse its failure by blaming the inconsequent emotions of the people. The policy of appeasement followed by the British Government during the thirties, for instance, is often defended on the grounds that any other course of action would only have been possible if Britain had first rearmed, but that rearmament was out of the question because of the sentimental opposition of the British people. Lord Baldwin, according to his biographer Mr. G. M. Young,[1] appreciated the weaknesses of British defences, foresaw the danger of war, had no confidence in the ability of members of the League of Nations to reach effective agreement for preserving the peace and was thus convinced of the need for British rearmament. He did not act on this conviction because, ever since his party had lost a by-election in 1933, he had also believed the pacifist sentiments of the British people to be so strong that:

> 'Supposing I had gone to the country and said that Germany was rearming and we must rearm, does anybody think that this pacific democracy would have rallied to that cry at that moment? I cannot think of anything that would have made the loss of the election from my point of view more certain.'[2]

This is not an altogether convincing excuse. Baldwin's entire career demonstrates his readiness to defy popular sentiment and to risk electoral disadvantage whenever he considered this desirable, not least in his stubborn and successful resistance to the General Strike of 1926. Few politicians of the period displayed greater skill or perseverance in converting opponents, inside the Conservative party or outside, to new and unwelcome ideas. If he shrank from this course over rearmament and foreign policy, the reason must be sought elsewhere than in the supposed existence of unalterably pacifist aspirations among the British people. Neither this episode nor the conduct in office of subsequent British governments can be invoked to justify the proposition that politicians are helpless slaves to the impulses of the electorate.

National aspirations are not evolved spontaneously, but

[1] G. M. Young, op. cit.
[2] G. M. Young, op. cit.

emerge from a dialogue between people and politicians in which most of the talking is done by the politicians. It is they who play the major part in the formulation of popular wishes and, if these seem more often to emerge in the form of vague sentiments than of consistently specific propositions, then politicians, rather than the people at large, must be assumed to prefer an imprecision that preserves their freedom of action.

Just how far this freedom of action can go may be illustrated by a comparison of certain points in the Conservative election manifesto of 1959 with the policies actually followed by the Conservative Government once returned to power. Similar contrasts, of course, could be drawn from any other recent election, but that of 1959 is particularly suitable because the then Prime Minister, Mr. Macmillan, announced at the outset that he had chosen the date for the election 'in the light of the world situation. Important international negotiations lie ahead. It is clearly right that the people should have the opportunity of deciding, as soon as practicable, who are to represent them in these negotiations.'[1]

This emphasis on popular choice, not of the issues to be negotiated, but of the persons to conduct the negotiations, was significant. It was to be echoed throughout the campaign and the section of the Labour Party manifesto devoted to international affairs was prefaced by the question 'Who Goes to the Summit?' and ended by claiming that 'hundreds of millions of people throughout the world' hoped this would be a Labour Prime Minister.

Nevertheless, the Conservative Party manifesto did make some specific proposals concerning nuclear testing and the Conservative Government did subsequently pursue these with some degree of success. It was the more general propositions in the manifesto which produced such a curious contrast between promise and performance.

[1] See D. E. Butler and R. Rose *The British General Election of 1959* (Macmillan 1960).

At the outset the manifesto declared:

> 'As for peace, it is of course the supreme purpose of all policy.'

Later it explained that this was to be achieved by the abolition of nuclear weapons and

> 'the reduction of the other weapons and armed forces to a level which will rule out the possibility of an aggressive war,'

but

> 'Meanwhile it remains vitally important to maintain our defensive alliances throughout the world.'

The experienced Conservative leaders who submitted these propositions for the endorsement of the electorate cannot really have regarded peace as the '*supreme* purpose of policy'; they must have realized that disarmament may reduce the destructiveness of war but cannot '*rule out*' its possibility (Britain could again be invaded by irregular levies of swordsmen in rowing-boats if all armaments were reduced to the level of a thousand years ago); they surely knew of considerations more '*vitally important*' than the maintenance of 'our defensive alliances throughout the world'.

The proof of these assertions lies in their actual conduct of affairs when in office. Peace was not, in any ordinary meaning of the English language, the supreme purpose of all policy when British forces were sent to Thailand in 1962 or, in much larger numbers and for actual fighting, to Borneo in 1963 and 1964. Fighting a small war may, it is sometimes argued, help to prevent a larger conflict, but this was never seriously suggested as the reason for resisting Indonesian 'confrontation' against Malaysia. Britain's treaty obligations and her supposed national interests were given priority (perhaps rightly – it is not the merits of the decision that are in question here) over the 'supreme purpose of all policy'.

Admittedly the defence of Malaysia reflected the 'vital

importance of maintaining our defensive alliances throughout the world', but there was to be no reaffirmation of this principle when India attacked our oldest ally, Portugal, in Goa; when Indonesia attacked our Dutch allies in New Guinea or when some of our allies in the South-East Asia Treaty Organization were sufficiently tactless to suggest the possible applicability of the Manila Treaty to Kashmir or Vietnam.

It would be unfair, however, to complain of the Conservative Government's failure to 'rule out the possibility of an aggressive war', an objective entirely on a par with 'stamping out crime'.

Here, however, were three national aspirations, duly submitted to the people and endorsed by the election of their proposers, which proved as irrelevant in practice as in theory. Similar results would undoubtedly have occurred if the Labour Party had won the election and attempted to

> 'substitute the rule of law and negotiated settlements for the power politics of conflicting blocs'

(an aspiration which irresistibly evokes the time-honoured retort of every schoolboy – 'you and who else?') or to act on their strange affirmation that

> 'one man one vote applies in all parts of the world.'

It was in 1932 that Sir Winston Churchill remarked:

> 'I cannot recall any time when the gap between the kind of words which statesmen used and what was actually happening in many countries was so great as it is now.'[1]

But his comment would have been equally applicable in any subsequent year. Unfortunately it was also Churchill who deprecated 'extravagant logic in doctrine'[2] and it would certainly be possible to quote many instances of his characteristically English parsimony in this direction.

[1] Winston Churchill, *Arms and the Covenant*, quoted in E. H. Carr, *The Twenty Years Crisis* (Macmillan 1940).

[2] Winston Churchill, *Step by Step* (Macmillan 1943).

Are we, therefore, to conclude that the entire concept of relevance is, as many politicians would undoubtedly contend, a hopelessly academic notion of no practical application to national aspirations in the field of foreign affairs? Must the British people really resign themselves to deciding merely 'who goes to the Summit?' without giving him more than the vaguest idea of what they want him to do at that eminence?

This is not a view which will survive unaltered a critical examination of the processes by which decisions are actually reached in the field of foreign affairs. A dispute arises and its nature is explained to the Foreign Secretary by his officials, who will also indicate which courses of action are open to the British Government and which (on assumptions to be discussed in subsequent chapters) would be best suited to British national interests and capacities. But it is the function of the Foreign Secretary himself – in conjunction with his ministerial colleagues and, occasionally, his parliamentary supporters as well – to define the extent to which decisions must be modified by national aspirations, by what the people want or, as it is sometimes put, by what they will stand. Lord Strang examines this process in detail, sometimes with a discernible tinge of regret at its necessity, in the authoritative chapter on 'The Formation and Control of Foreign Policy' in his book *The Diplomatic Career*. No one with experience in these matters can doubt that public opinion does actually influence Ministers in reaching decisions in the field of foreign policy, but the question posed at the beginning of this chapter still awaits an answer: 'how do those concerned with the shaping and execution of foreign policy identify the particular national aspirations which they ought to take into account?'

We have already seen that, except for the broadest and vaguest of sentiments, there is seldom anything approaching unanimity in such aspirations. It is also evident that many aspirations that could plausibly be held to enjoy majority support are irrelevant in theory and disregarded in practice. If Ministers are nevertheless influenced by public opinion, there must be some useful residue after so much has been discarded as either controversial or meaningless. Perhaps the clue lies in the phrase earlier attributed to an imaginary Foreign Secretary: 'what the people will stand'.

It has often been argued, particularly by students of the electoral process, that the British people possess a clearer conception of what they do *not* want than of what they do. They vote against, rather than for. This is a particularly important concept in the field of foreign affairs, where the wishes of the people are not only of personal importance to Ministers desirous of eventual re-election, but constitute an essential component of the national capacity. This is to be the subject of a subsequent chapter, but may be here briefly defined as the combination of resources available to a British Government when endeavouring to get their own way in a dispute with another Government. All these resources are, in the last resort, dependent on the will of the people to put them into operation, not only in the extremity of war, but in every stage of a dispute, in which one of the most familiar opening moves is for a British representative abroad to receive instructions to tell a foreign government that 'British public opinion is gravely concerned'. Even this manœuvre will lose any value it might otherwise have possessed if it is obvious to the foreign government in question from the B.B.C. and the British Press that large sections of British public opinion are in fact opposed to the policy of the Government of the day.

To any British Foreign Secretary, therefore, the practical test of a projected policy, so far as national aspirations are concerned, must be: will it arouse such opposition as either to endanger my own authority or the credibility of my representations to foreign governments?

The Hoare–Laval agreement of 1935 was probably the

most clear-cut and dramatic instance of a British Government changing course in response to public opposition, but there have been other occasions when this factor has certainly played a part: in hastening the end of British intervention in Russia during the early twenties; in abruptly modifying the tone of Mr. Neville Chamberlain's response to the German seizure of Prague in March 1939; in persuading the Churchill Government to oppose collaboration with Admiral Darlan in November 1942. In this last case, Churchill specifically says: 'I was conscious of the rising tide of opinion around me' but also 'I considered their attitude unreasonable'.[1] He defended vigorously the decisions already taken, but he nevertheless urged upon the United States Government the need for a change in policy and quoted the reaction of British public opinion as the justification for such a change.

And, for every occasion when British policy has, after its adoption, been reversed or significantly modified in response to public opposition, there have been many more, most of them yet to be identified and established by historians, in which the expectation of public opposition has prevented a policy from ever being adopted at all. Sometimes, as has been suggested was the case with Lord Baldwin, this expectation of opposition may have been more of an excuse for inaction than a single and sufficient cause. If the need for action had seemed to him as compelling as it had over tariffs, the General Strike or India, he might have argued his case and won it, but there is no reason to doubt that public opinion played at least some part in his abstention.

Since 1945, too, there have been various occasions on which the negative forces of public opinion have exerted their influence. British withdrawal from Palestine in 1948 was not a decision which followed naturally from the policy previously pursued by the British Government, nor did it preserve what that government had described as

[1] Winston Churchill, *The Hinge of Fate*, Chapter XXXV (Cassell 1951).

important British interests. To the United Nations, who opposed the British decision, this was justified on the grounds that 'His Majesty's Government were not themselves prepared to undertake the task of imposing a policy in Palestine by force of arms'.[1] But this was just what the Attlee Government had been attempting for the previous three years. It is what they were again to attempt, sometimes with greater success, in other parts of the world. It was certainly not from pacifist principle that they abandoned the attempt in 1948 and it is highly probable that this British Government decided as they did because they believed that continuance of their previous policy would no longer command the necessary minimum of support from the British people. The fact that this change of policy took place against the expressed wishes of the United Nations is an interesting commentary on Lord Attlee's declaration, two and a half years previously: 'The United Nations Organization must become the overriding factor in foreign policy.'[2]

The negative factor seems also to have been preponderant in the long series of decisions whereby successive British Governments abandoned British rule in so many overseas territories. It would be difficult to argue that there existed any overwhelming enthusiasm among the British people for all these transfers of sovereignty and the earlier stages of this process, which took place under a Labour Government, were hotly opposed by the Conservative Party. Yet the process was continued by Sir Winston Churchill and his Conservative successors in office. At times, for particular reasons and for brief periods, it was resisted: in Cyprus, in Kenya, in Aden. But ultimately withdrawal took place, often in the very circumstances previously declared by Ministers to be intolerable, because the Government of the day had come to

[1] British White Paper: 'Palestine: Termination of the Mandate: 15 May 1948.'

[2] H.M.S.O. Attlee, op. cit., Chapter XX.

realize that the British people were reluctant to continue the struggle, or, as Mr. Duncan Sandys once put it, because 'we British have lost the will to govern'.[1] Many of these decisions, admittedly, were justified at the time on other grounds and it may be years before the importance of this negative force of public opinion can be fully established to the satisfaction of the historian. But, as a working hypothesis, it does seem to explain more convincingly than any of the official apologia why the vital national interests or the overriding moral principles which, at any given moment, sent British troops to fight and die in these overseas territories had so entirely disappeared when the time came, a year or two later, to withdraw and to hand over power to the very leaders whose incapacity or turpitude had been so hotly denounced.

Finally, as the most recent of these instances, there is the case of Rhodesia, where one strand of usually tacit agreement united politicians otherwise deeply divided: British troops should not be employed to enforce the policy of the British Government.

Mr. Woodhouse, in the chapter on 'Party Politics' in his *British Foreign Policy Since the Second World War*[2] also comes to 'the conclusion that no British Government since the war has been the undivided master of its own foreign policy' and identifies as the three types of question liable to provoke dissensions:

> 'Which policy is likely to preserve peace and which to lead to war?
> Secondly, which policy is morally right?
> Thirdly, what policy can the country's economy afford?'

As a member of parliament, Mr. Woodhouse is more concerned, as he makes clear in his book, with dissension among the politicians themselves than with the deeper

[1] Quoted in Anthony Sampson, *Macmillan: A Study in Ambiguity* (Allen Lane, The Penguin Press 1967).

[2] C. M. Woodhouse, *British Foreign Policy Since The Second Word War* (Hutchinson 1961).

springs of public opinion, but all three of his questions are ultimately liable to attract the decisively negative reply: we don't want to fight; we don't want to put up with that, we don't want to pay for this. Theoretically it may be just as hard to prove the existence of widespread popular support for a negative as for a positive aspiration, but, in practice, it often seems that Ministers are more easily convinced of opposition to any particular course of action than they are of support. It is also harder to dispute the relevance of a negative: 'we want peace' may mean many things; 'we don't want to fight' is considerably clearer.

It is also in giving vent to negative aspirations that the balance of public opinion is occasionally redressed in favour of sections of the people generally afforded little opportunity for the effective expression of their views on matters of foreign policy: the young and the working-classes. In the dialogue between people and politicians, the people are usually represented by the small minority of the articulate: those who can formulate opinions, who have access to the organs of mass communication, who know politicians or officials, who possess influence. When the British Government are urged to take some positive step or to adopt some particular policy, the initiative – and often the sole impulse – normally comes from people of a certain age and position, from what is sometimes termed 'the Establishment', even if this may be the established opposition.

In practice, however, governments are often disposed to ignore positive aspirations of this kind, even when these are put forward by persons claiming to act in a representative capacity. Labour governments, for instance, have not always proved responsive to motions on foreign policy passed by the annual conference of the Trades Union Congress. Perhaps Ministers have a shrewd idea of how many trade unionists were actually consulted, how many factory or dockside meetings had actually been held, before the block votes were cast on Vietnam or Rhodesia.

But, when the cry was 'Hands off Russia' and this

negative aspiration was visibly backed by trade union interference with ships loading munitions for use against the Red Army, this negative aspiration was effective. The most conservative of British governments seldom cares to pursue a dispute with a foreign power against the expressed opposition of the British working-class.

Young men, too, may not exercise much influence on policy by assembling in their thousands to call for nuclear disarmament, but governments are acutely sensitive to any suggestion that the young might refuse military service. This means of pressure has not so far been effectively exerted in support of a negative aspiration in Britain, but the merest hint of it – in the famous resolution of the Oxford Union in 1933 'That this House refuses to fight for King and country' – created a far greater impression, both at home and abroad, than any of the positive aspirations voiced since 1945 by much larger numbers of young people.

Negative aspirations are naturally most likely to be effective when, as in the two instances quoted, they are addressed to the fundamental issue of 'yield or fight' and are backed by the threat of withholding co-operation. But they can be effective in other fields as well.

Woodhouse, writing both as a scholar of international affairs and as a practising politician, discusses another aspect of the negative force of public opinion in his chapter on the 'Changing Patterns' of British foreign policy. He examines – and treats as a blind alley – the record of British attitudes towards European union between 1945 and 1960. He points out that the idea of a united Europe appears to offer a solution to one of the main problems confronting the British people: the extent to which their relative importance in the world had declined since 1939. Yet – and what he wrote in 1960 still seemed valid in 1967 – 'There has never been any sentiment in favour of Britain's participation in European union, except among a few enthusiasts.' Indeed, all the arguments put forward since his book was published in

January 1961, first by a Conservative Government against Labour opposition, then by a Labour Government with Conservative support, in favour of British entry to the Common Market have been based on considerations of national interest rather than national aspiration. Even when both political parties had pronounced in favour of this course, it would have been hard to argue that any overwhelmingly pro-European sentiment was discernible among the British people. It was rather that popular opposition to the idea of closer association with Europe – advocated by Churchill as early as 1946 – had at last declined to a point at which a British Government could propose – at least five years too late – a course of action so long urged by some of their professional advisers and – in opposition – by leading politicians. Once again, it is not the merits of this decision which are in question here: only the power of public opinion to force its postponement.

National aspirations, therefore, can seldom be identified with certainty, are essentially emotional in character and are often irrelevant to the shaping and execution of foreign policy. Nevertheless British governments believe them to exist, invoke them at elections and in support of their policy and, often though by no means always, allow them to influence actual decisions. This influence is most likely to be effective when it is negative and operates so as to prevent or delay the adoption or continuance of a particular course of action.

These are slender conclusions to draw from so much argument, particularly from an analysis which has deliberately neglected such fascinating digressions as the influence on aspirations of class, age and sectional interests. But this chapter will have served its purpose if, even while making the major assumption that there is such a thing as public opinion, it has cleared away a few misconceptions and isolated some of the basic tests to be applied by those concerned with the shaping and execution of British foreign policy. Is public opinion, so far as it can be ascertained, evenly divided or is there a preponderant trend? Is it based on sentiment or interest? Is it relevant? Does it offer a guide only in the initial phases of dispute or is there any coherent view on the ultimate issues of yielding or fighting? Finally, there is the decisive question, which is not 'what do the people want?', but 'what will they put up with?' In the last resort the task of the British Government, when weighing the possible reactions of British public opinion to issues of foreign policy, is to decide what the British people can be expected to oppose.

It is not for a book expressly devoted to seeking, not answers, but the appropriate questions, to prescribe what methods should be employed by British governments to resolve any doubts they may entertain on this crucial issue. Instead the last word might be left to a politician not always cited with complete approval. In describing one of Lord Baldwin's more successful decisions his biographer writes:

> 'I once said to Baldwin, "I believe you were the only man on Friday who knew what the House of Commons would be thinking on Monday." He replied, with a smile half shy and half triumphant, "I have always believed in the week-end. But how they do it I don't know. I suppose they talk to the station-master."'[1]

[1] G. M. Young, op. cit.

3

NATIONAL INTERESTS

'It should be forbidden by law for members of the Government to use the phrase "in the national interest".'

Lord Radcliffe[1]

THE analysis of national interests as a factor in the development of foreign policy presents problems of greater difficulty and complexity than any encountered in relation to national aspirations. An aspiration is normally expressed in words; these generally indicate some kind of purpose and, when uttered, provide the aspiration with an objective existence. It was not difficult, for instance, to interpret the meaning of 'better red than dead', nor did the significance of this slogan depend on the process of reasoning by which it had been reached. Once uttered, it existed and all that was necessary was to decide whether it commanded sufficient popular support to constitute a 'national aspiration' requiring to be taken into account in the shaping of policy.

The 'national interest', on the other hand, is a theoretical concept, supposedly of an axiomatic character, serving as the basis for a chain of argument which, when applied to a given set of circumstances, indicates a particular conclusion. It does not matter whether this conclusion enjoys popular support. Indeed, the national interest is often invoked to justify unpopular policies, the assumption being that argument can demonstrate that these policies correspond to real needs, as opposed to sentimental impulses. In practice, however, the complete

[1] Quoted in *The Observer*, 24 December 1967.

chain of argument is seldom stated. At best, the nature of the problem is expounded, alternative courses of action are examined and their results predicted and one of these courses is then preferred as that most likely to bring about a state of affairs judged, by precept or precedent, to be 'in the national interest'.

During the prolonged controversy over British retention of nuclear weapons, for instance, one of the questions at issue was the effect on British international influence. Some contended that this would be diminished, others that it would be increased, if Britain possessed no nuclear weapons of her own. Neither side found it necessary to explain why it was in the national interest for Britain to exert influence abroad, still less to preface their argument by a definition of the national interest and to deduce from the terms of this definition that influence was indeed desirable. This was taken for granted and, in any discussion of foreign policy, as in the ordinary affairs of everyday life, assumptions of similar magnitude are inevitable. Men and women come, by precept, by example or by experience, to regard certain objectives and certain forms of conduct as 'better', 'more advantageous' or 'more desirable' than others and they sometimes act accordingly. They have neither the time nor the inclination to examine the philosophic basis of their assumptions. Only, perhaps, when these are questioned by their adolescent children, do they realize that other assumptions are possible and that the generally accepted rules governing everyday conduct are no longer the same in 1967 as they were in 1937. It is at this moment that even the most pragmatic of parents may find himself driven to justify his working rules of 'good behaviour' by arguments based on some abstract conception of 'good'.

The working rules of foreign policy are equally susceptible to change. Today, for instance, the objective of 'British maritime supremacy' seems as irrelevant as the Protestant Cause or the British claim to the throne of

France. Yet the doctrine of maritime supremacy not only dominated British foreign policy during the nineteenth century, but was a major cause of British participation in the First World War and at least a contributary factor to British involvement in the Second. For generations it was the basis of British policy and a seemingly inseparable component of the national interest. At other periods official opinion has attached similar importance to the balance of power in Europe, to the maintenance of Empire, to collective security, to Western unity or to the defence of the Free World. When decisions had to be taken, or policies shaped, they were tested for their conformity not only with the facts of the situation, but also with the ruling doctrine of the day, which was regarded as expressing the national interest in the form most suited to contemporary needs. If the doctrine itself had to be defended, this was done by instancing the practical advantages of its application or the unfortunate consequences of its neglect. Thus, what was theoretically only an intermediate stage in a chain of reasoning leading from some basic conception of the national interest to an actual decision became, in practice, the central focus of the entire argument. Decisions were taken because they conformed to the doctrine, which was justified by the results of previous decisions.

The convenience of such working formulae as a rule of thumb guide to swift decision is obvious, but so are the dangers. Whereas any particular doctrine may originally have been rationally derived from a valid conception of the national interest, it soon acquires an apparently intrinsic truth, thus enabling acceptance of the doctrine to outlast the actual duration of its compatibility either with external circumstance or with the national interest. It has already been argued, for instance, that the decision to use force in the Suez crisis of 1956 was prompted by a doctrine – the need for early resistance to aggressive dictators – evolved in response to the international situation of twenty years earlier. The unfortunate consequences of this decision suggest that, whether or not the doctrine accurately reflected the national interest in 1936, it no longer did so in 1956. It is thus arguable that, if the courses of action open to the British Government in 1956 had been tested against some basic conception of the national interest rather than against an obsolete derivation of this conception, a different decision might have been reached. Alternatively, if more importance had been attached to the theoretical basis of British foreign policy, there might have existed a more up-to-date doctrine which more nearly expressed the national interest in the altered circumstances of 1956. As it was, the chain of reasoning seems to have been not merely incomplete, but actually circular. It was in the national interest to resist this aggressive dictator because experience was supposed to have shown that it was not in the national interest not to have resisted another aggressive dictator. The missing term was a definition of the national interest.

The purpose of this chapter, therefore, is to isolate the intrinsic concept of the national interest from its derivations and to define it in terms not dependant for their validity on any particular combination of material circumstances. To the extent that this could be achieved, the result would be a single premise capable of leading, through the varying chains of reasoning required by different circumstances, to useful conclusions on the practical requirements, in any given situation, of the national interest.

It would, of course, be consistent with the line of argument so far employed, if this definition were itself to be rationally derived from some even more fundamental axiom. The search for ultimate truth, however, has caused too many illustrious footsteps to stray for it even to be attempted by the present author. The results, if any, might also prove mainly applicable to a more perfect condition of humanity than that now represented by the British nation. It accordingly seems preferable to seek this basic definition by deduction from the actual policies, decisions and declarations of British governments. These have naturally been powerfully influenced by different combinations of material circumstances, by varying national aspirations and capacities, and even by the personal character and abilities of those directly concerned. Yet, if such a thing as the national interest exists at all, it ought to be possible to discern a single strand of motive as a common factor underlying even the most apparently diverse of decisions. If such a concept can be isolated and can survive such tests as common sense may indicate, then this, it will be suggested, is what governments actually mean, whether or not they realize it themselves, when they speak of the national interest.

Before embarking on this difficult journey across debatable ground, there is one entirely legitimate cause of confusion that should first be disposed of. Among the many possible meanings of the word 'interest', there are two which are directly relevant and require to be carefully distinguished. A man can have an interest in a factory in the sense that he owns part of it; or he may have an interest in the factory's continued prosperity, because it is on this that his job depends. The second kind of interest provides a specific motive not necessarily inherent in the first: the part-owner of a factory may only want to make a tax-loss on its operation or to pull it down. Similar distinctions apply in international affairs. In 1951 the Anglo-Iranian Oil Company, in which the British Government held a majority of the shares, owned an oil refinery at Abadan. The British nation thus had an interest in the refinery to such an extent that it could properly be described as a British national interest. On the other hand, when this British national interest was menaced by the Government of Iran, the British Government of the day rejected the use of force to defend Abadan as being contrary to the national interest.

It is with the latter conception of national interest as a motive force for policy that this chapter is primarily concerned. When it is necessary to refer to the other kind of interest – in property overseas or the income it produces, or in the welfare of British subjects abroad – the term 'British interest' or 'British interests' will be employed to distinguish these concrete examples of a particular interest from the general abstraction of 'the national interest'.

This may strike some readers as a needlessly elaborate and ponderous approach to a concept often regarded as being no less susceptible of direct apprehension than 'red' or 'blue'. Many would even argue that the nature of the national interest is less controversial and thus easier to identify than almost any national aspiration. This is certainly the assumption of those who invoke the ritual formula, 'in the national interest', to hush the clamour of party dispute by appealing to concepts supposedly more enduring, more important and more generally accepted than those customarily argued among politicians. On this view the national interest is at once the material basis of patriotism and its *raison d'être*: a concept apart from politics and above them. Indeed, to those who regard the national interest as capable of intuitive perception, its analysis in terms of political theory may seem no less irrelevant than outrageous. Although they may occasionally suspect a particular Minister of intoning the sacred phrase in order to escape from a dilemma or to assist a secular cause, it is only the unworthiness of the priest that is blamed: the authority of the Oracle remains.

But, even if this sceptical generation could accept the idea of a national interest divorced from politics and capable of direct apprehension, who could be judged fit to read the sacred books? Once, it seemed, their natural custodians were the Admiralty, the Foreign Office, even, to the romantic, the Secret Service, perhaps, to the more prosaically inclined, the Bank of England. But all these institutions are now somewhat blown upon and it would be hard to find a generally acceptable High Priest of the national interest. Certainly no Prime Minister or Foreign

Secretary of the last twenty years has commanded universal or continuous respect in this exacting rôle. If the national interest is above politics, its interpretation is not.

Yet the national interest is still constantly invoked to justify practical decisions without anything approaching the open and unrestrained controversy by which national aspirations are, however imperfectly, daily tested in public debate. The national interest is the argument of committees, of telephone conversations, of quick meetings across the luncheon table, of the Cabinet Room. When it is used in public, the test most commonly applied is that of sincerity: does the Minister really believe what he is saying or is he thinking of votes or dividends? Occasionally it may be suggested that his facts are wrong or his predictions mistaken, seldom that his premises are defective.

Of all the considerations relevant to foreign policy the national interest is most likely to be taken for granted as part of that 'large area of common ground' which, as Lord Strang has said, 'does not need to be explained or demonstrated'.[1] Yet, whenever time or opportunity are afforded for discussion, it soon becomes evident that the national interest can be differently interpreted. The question of British entry to the European Common Market, for instance, has been exhaustively debated for years and most of the arguments employed have been of the kind previously described as based on interest rather than aspiration: whether, to what extent and how soon such a step would confer material advantages on the British people? This debate has not only revealed the widest divergences in factual predictions – the effect on the balance of payments or the cost of living – but also on the fundamental issue of what is or is not in the national interest. One of the advantages claimed for British entry to the Common Market, for instance, is that the spur of competition would stimulate the best British industries to greater efficiency while driving the worst to bankruptcy.

[1] *The Diplomatic Career*, op. cit.

But in what sense is it a national interest that even inefficient British firms should become bankrupt and their employees lose their jobs? An argument against entry, on the other hand, is that the British people would have to pay more for their food. But, does this matter if they also have to pay less taxes to subsidize British farmers and if the latter then find it economical to expand production, thus ensuring that the increased expenditure of British consumers is received by British farmers? These, and many other arguments, the merits of which are irrelevant to this book, all turn on assumptions that entry to the Common Market will benefit some sections of the British people, cause loss to others, but, sooner or later, will or will not prove of material advantage to 'the national interest'. But what is the 'national interest'? Is it better that efficient British firms should flourish abundantly or that the weaker brethren should be protected against foreign competition? Would greater self-sufficiency in agricultural production be an adequate compensation for higher food prices? These are not questions which can be resolved simply by reaching agreement on statistical projections. Their answers depend on theoretical concepts of what constitutes the national interest as opposed to the conflicting interests of different sections of the British people.

British entry to the European Common Market is, however, an exceptional issue in the field of foreign affairs, because opposition, first at home and later abroad, has so delayed action as to permit ample time for discussion. This discussion has considerably clarified the ideas of both the supporters and the opponents of entry to the Common Market. In so far as common ground exists between them, it would probably be fair to say that this was very different in 1967 from the common ground of 1961 and that six years of debate have appreciably modified almost everyone's conception of the national interest in this issue. Certainly the attitudes of both the major political parties, and the arguments employed by their leaders, have altered. Some of those who, in 1961, contended that this step would be against the national interest, now take the opposite view. Is this due solely to the change effected by time in the objective facts of the situation or does it also reflect an altered conception of the national interest?

The great majority of decisions in the field of foreign affairs do not benefit by such prolonged and exhaustive opportunities for analysis and discussion. Many of them have to be taken without any public debate at all, some of them in a matter of hours. Nearly always these decisions are taken on the basis of assumptions concerning the national interest, assumptions which are neither discussed nor even explained. As Lord Strang has pointed out, 'the number of ways in which the national interest can be damaged by foreign action is legion'. Nobody could dispute his conclusion that 'to find the best way to meet each of them will call for an individual exercise, separately conducted'.[1] But it is equally obvious that this exercise will, in practice, be devoted primarily to establishing the facts of the particular situation, together with the various courses of action open to the British Government. The choice between these different courses must, to a considerable extent, depend on prior assumptions of a theoretical character concerning the nature of the 'national interest'.

A problem that arises almost daily, concerns the action required of the British Government when the persons, property or 'interests' of British subjects have been injured by the action, or by the neglect, of a foreign government. Such injuries can be of varying gravity: a British tourist may have been imprisoned for a few hours or a whole community exposed to mob violence; a British firm may have suffered discrimination in the grant of import licences, or a major oil company may have been expropriated. The circumstances of each case and the practical considerations affecting the decision of the British Government will probably be very different. But, arising

[1] *The Diplomatic Career.*

from every incident, there will be one primary question: is this the private misfortune of one or more British subjects or is the national interest involved? In the former case, the local British representative will endeavour to assist his aggrieved compatriots to the extent that the laws and administrative practice of the foreign State permit; in the latter the British Government may treat the incident as the subject of a dispute with the foreign State concerned. The choice will be determined only in part by the particular circumstances of the case: certain general, though often unspoken, assumptions will also exercise great influence. Lord Palmerston, for instance, regarded the national interest as automatically involved in disputes between British subjects and foreign governments and seems to have been actuated by this general principle rather than by the merits of the case in carrying to such extremes his celebrated defence of Don Pacifico. Admittedly this was in 1850 but, as late as 1933, the British Government imposed an embargo on imports from the Soviet Union in order to secure the release of two British subjects sentenced to imprisonment by a Soviet court. This measure produced the desired results, but in recent years many British subjects have suffered graver injuries at the hands of foreign governments much more vulnerable to pressure than that of the Soviet Union without any corresponding reaction from the British Government. In many of these cases the inaction of the British Government was justified on seemingly pragmatic grounds: any form of retaliation would have been damaging to other British interests. But these arguments only masked an altered conception of the national interest. If an individual British subject has been injured by a foreign government, the cost of coercing that government into providing redress is almost bound to be as disproportionate, considered in isolation and 'on the merits of the case', as that of bringing a domestic murderer to justice. Where it has nevertheless been attempted, the reasoning has often been that a successful act of coercion will bring long-term benefits by deterring the same or other foreign governments from similarly injuring British subjects in future. The choice required is not only between the immediate disadvantages of coercion and its potential benefits in the long term, but also between the interests of those British subjects who seldom, if ever, travel abroad and those who spend much of their lives in foreign parts. Which is more conducive to the national interest: to deter foreign governments from molesting the small minority of British subjects at their mercy or to spare their more numerous compatriots the extra risk and expense that such a policy would entail?

These are over-simplified examples, because they neglect the influence on such decisions of national aspirations and national capacities, but they point the way to the first of the fundamental questions to be considered in this chapter: whose is the national interest? The obvious answer – that of the British people as a whole – will not do, because we have seen that, in great issues as in small everyday incidents, it is possible for different sections of the British people to have conflicting interests. The answer of the Marxist – the national interest is in practice interpreted as the interest of the ruling class – deserves more attention. It is not essential to accept the Marxist conception of class (a word which, in English, has confusing overtones unrelated to the means of production) to agree that Britain, in common with other nation-states, is an oligarchy. Ordinary observation confirms that only a small minority of the population have any regular opportunity – or inclination – to influence the decisions and policies of the Government. In so far as this small minority have a common interest distinct from that of the majority of the population, it is this interest which consciously or unconsciously, is likely to be represented and accepted as the national interest.

One such interest is the maintenance of the existing social order. Someone capable of influencing the decisions and policies of the Government necessarily occupies a position of relative power and privilege. Such persons may wish to modify the social structure or to improve their own status within it: they seldom wish, once they have their feet on the rungs of the ladder, to knock it away before, like Mao Tse Tung, they have climbed to the top. Within any society, therefore, the ruling class, if this term is strictly defined to mean those capable of influencing the decisions and policies of the Government, are likely to have a greater common interest than the rest of the population in the maintenance of the existing social order. This interest can easily be interpreted as a national interest affecting foreign policy. The rulers of the Soviet Union, for instance, have long suspected many foreign governments (now including that of China) of a desire to overthrow the existing social order in the Soviet Union. Plans for combating these supposed intentions thus exercise an important influence on Soviet foreign policy. Successive British governments have similarly suspected the Soviet Government of wishing to promote revolution in Britain, perhaps with rather more reason, given official Soviet pronouncements on the subject, and have shaped their policy accordingly.

Interests of this kind can, of course, extend well beyond the actual rulers of Britain. Anyone who benefits by the existing order of things and fears that any likely change might leave him worse off tends to become a supporter of the *status quo* and to identify this with the national interest. This kind of 'conservatism' can have very varied effects on the shaping of the 'national interest' as a concept influencing foreign policy. On many occasions since 1945, for instance, sections of the Labour Party have contended that a particular course of foreign policy would be against the national interest, because it would entail expenditure prejudicial to the maintenance of a Welfare State. This was, in essence, the issue on which three Ministers resigned from the Labour Government in April 1951. On other occasions sections of the Conservative Party have advocated, over the Congo for instance, policies represented as being in the national interest because they would ensure a continued flow of dividends to Britain from foreign investments abroad. To some extent, of course, these dividends would benefit the national economy and thus, indirectly, the population as a whole. Nevertheless, the benefits to a small minority would be disproportionate and one of the justifications for identifying the interests of this minority with 'the national interest' would be that the existing social order was thereby upheld: the power of the State was being exerted to preserve the right to private property.

Indeed, because overseas dividends confer much greater benefits on the few individuals who actually receive them than on the mass of the population, there is obviously a particularly strong 'class interest' in a foreign policy intended not only to defend identifiably British interests abroad, but also to maintain conditions in foreign countries favourable to the free flow of dividends to Britain. These objectives are less readily accepted as forming part of the 'national interest' by those without any prospect of personal benefit, either directly or through reaffirmation of the sanctity of unearned income. On the other hand, although the cost to the nation as a whole of preserving a particular 'British interest' abroad may be disproportionate to its value, it is sometimes argued that only a consistent policy of defending all sources of overseas revenue can prevent the loss of so much income that the cumulative effect on the national economy would be reflected in a lower standard of living for the mass of the population. In 1956, for instance, when the defence of 'British interests' abroad was a controversial issue in foreign policy, interest, profits, etc., received from abroad were estimated at £667 million, enough to pay for nearly a sixth of all British imports. This argument in turn invites the retort that assets abroad, and the revenue they earn, are inherently precarious; that it is contrary to the national interest to rely on them and that the affairs of Britain, even the British social structure, should be so rearranged as to free Britain from dependence on foreigners for anything but current transactions. According to this theory it is consonant with the national interest to rely on imported food and raw materials only to the extent that these can be purchased by exports of British manufactures. We can depend on foreigners selling us wheat because they need our motor-cars in exchange: we cannot depend on their continuing to send us wheat if this represents only the payment of interest on money borrowed – and spent – long ago.

The reader can himself pursue these arguments and counter-arguments to his own satisfaction: their only purpose here is to demonstrate the extent to which the concept of the national interest can be coloured by the interests of a particular class. Nevertheless, even if it is admitted that the ruling class play the major part in defining the national interest, as this is interpreted in practice, and that this definition is strongly influenced by the particular interests of that class, it may be doubted whether these factors are sufficient to explain the whole of the complicated process whereby this abstruse and controversial concept contributes to the formation of foreign policy. The British Government have been involved in many disputes where it is difficult to discern the maintenance of the existing social order or the material interests of the ruling class as a sufficient motive.

The Second World War is a case in point. The outcome of this war, though nominally a victory for Britain, was manifestly detrimental to the interests of the British ruling class. Indeed, it has often been argued that this outcome was sufficiently predictable to prompt the British ruling class to do all in their power to avoid war and, hence, to pursue a policy of appeasement at the risk of having eventually to fight in less favourable circumstances. In particular, it has been suggested that one alternative to appeasement – a policy of alliance with the Soviet Union against Germany – was expressly excluded because of the threat this implied, not to Britain as a whole, but to the existing British social structure and to the interests of the British ruling class.

Lord Baldwin, for instance, privately justified appeasement not only as a response to popular aspirations, but also because 'crushing Germany with the aid of Russia ... would probably only result in Germany going Bolshevik',[1] a prospect more to be feared than the activity of Nazi Germany. Sir Harold Nicolson, himself very much a member of the ruling class, often comments in his *Diaries* on the prevalence of such views. On 6 June 1938, for instance, he says:

> 'People of the governing classes think only of their own fortunes, which means hatred of the Reds. This creates a perfectly artificial but at present most effective secret bond between ourselves and Hitler.'[2]

The historical validity of this controversial theory lies beyond the scope of this book or the competence of its author. But, if it is accepted for the sake of argument, it gives rise to a most interesting question. If the maintenance of their privileges was the primary motive of the British ruling class and if this was regarded as more compatible with German territorial expansion than with an Anglo-Soviet alliance against Germany, why was this conception of the National interest rejected from the start by such typical members of the ruling class as Sir Winston Churchill and Lord Vansittart? Even more significantly, why did the Chamberlain Government, the arch exponents of appeasement, suddenly alter their attitude and court war with Germany by their guarantee to Poland in March 1939?

[1] Remarks to the Cabinet on 11 March 1936, as quoted in the *Sunday Times* of 31 December 1967.

[2] Harold Nicolson, *Diaries and Letters 1930–39* (Collins 1966).

> 'History' [as Churchill later commented] 'may be scoured and ransacked to find a parallel to this sudden and complete reversal of five or six years' policy of easy-going placatory appeasement, and its transformation almost overnight into a readiness to accept an obviously imminent war on far worse conditions and on the greatest scale.'[1]

German threats to Poland, after all, not only tended to move German military strength farther away from Britain, but also increased the likelihood of that conflict between Germany and the Soviet Union so often represented as the undeclared objective of the British ruling class during the period of their support for the policy of appeasement. Logically, we might suppose, this was the moment to reassure Germany that she had nothing to fear from Britain, thus encouraging the eastward German march to continue from Poland to the Soviet Union and the final elimination of this twenty-year-old threat to the privileges of the British ruling class. If this had really been Chamberlain's objective, there was surely nothing in Hitler's seizure of Prague to justify such an abrupt change of course by the British Government.

It is accordingly necessary to look for a conception of the national interest capable of explaining Chamberlain's policy both before and after the guarantee to Poland of 31 March 1939, to say nothing of the different attitudes throughout adopted by other sections of the ruling class. Perhaps this can be found in the proposition that the national interest resides, first and foremost, in the preservation of the independence and authority of the nation-state. In its emotional overtones of nationalism, patriotism or chauvinism, this may be regarded as an aspiration, but, in its central core, it is an interest of very wide application. To begin with, it offers a modification of the theory of class interest that brings this much more closely into line with observable historical trends. Although the privileges

[1] Churchill, *The Gathering Storm*, Chapter XIX (Cassell 1948).

of the ruling class, being based on wealth, are cosmopolitan and, in so far as this wealth is transferable, are to some extent independent of the nation-state, their power is not. And power, to those persons most capable of influencing governments, generally offers a stronger incentive than privilege. Those desirous of attributing to Chamberlain and his supporters motives based on class-interest can thus argue that, up to March 1939, they saw as the main foreign threat to their power and privileges the influence of the Soviet Union. It was Hitler's repudiation of the Munich bargain with Chamberlain by seizing Prague that convinced the British ruling class that there were no foreseeable limits to Hitler's ambition and that the Churchillian bogey – the eventual subjugation of the British nation-state by Germany – actually represented a more immediate threat to their class than revolution inspired by the growing influence of the Soviet Union.

Moreover, once the national interest is regarded as the expression of a common interest in the maintenance of the nation-state, it becomes easier to explain many other seeming anomalies. So far as aspirations went, for instance, the Labour Party were hostile to Germany before 1939 and favoured friendship with the Soviet Union after 1945. Yet the pre-war Labour Opposition consistently opposed military preparations against Germany, whereas the post-war Labour Government took military precautions against the Soviet Union. Even in opposition the attitude of the Labour Party on questions of defence and foreign policy has, since 1951, seemed closer to that of post-war Conservative governments than to the attitude adopted by the Labour Party before 1939. This can be explained in many ways, of which it is not necessarily the most cynical to say that participation in government or its prospect (which can scarcely have seemed very imminent to the Labour Party before 1939) greatly increases the importance attached by politicians to the maintenance of the nation-state. Even the most personally disinterested of Socialists could reasonably argue that a nation-state becomes more deserving of maintenance once there is a prospect of its being ruled by Socialists. This has certainly been the attitude adopted by the Communist Party of the Soviet Union so far as their own country is concerned. An alternative argument might even be that domestic changes since 1945 have increased the membership of the ruling class in Britain and made this membership much less dependent on the possession of wealth, so that the Labour party are now no less a party of the ruling class than their Conservative opponents.

But it is not necessary for a British subject to belong, even on the broadest definition, to the ruling class, in order to have some interest in maintaining the nation-state. Anyone surveying the course of events throughout the world since 1945 might reasonably conclude that relatively few nation-states had managed to ensure a better existence for the majority of their citizens than that enjoyed during the same period by the British people. Moreover, except for those few British subjects who choose to emigrate or for the tiny handful who may regard themselves as having rendered services to a foreign government deserving of reward from that government, the mass of the British people have no choice in the matter. Those discontented with their treatment at the hands of a British Government can seldom have any rational grounds for expecting better treatment from a foreign government. Members of the British Communist Party, for instance, doubtless believe that Britain could be better governed by themselves than by other British political parties, but few of them are likely to want Britain to become one of the constituent republics of the Soviet Union and to be governed by Russians. The common language and the common traditions created by shared membership of a long-established nation-state do in fact create a common interest among the majority of its inhabitants. Some of them may dislike the existing social order and strive towards its modification or even transformation, but they are seldom presented with any practical alternative to the maintenance of the nation-state.

It is, of course, this question of a practical alternative that has been the heart of the debate over British entry to the Common Market. Although nobody suggests that this would lead, in the foreseeable future, to the extinction of the British nation-state, there would undoubtedly be some restriction on the freedom of action of the British Government. At first sight this may seem inconsistent with the earlier suggestion that this issue was being argued in terms of the national interest. If this requires the maintenance of the independence and authority of the nation-state, how can the national interest be invoked to support a course of action necessarily entailing the acceptance of restrictions on this independence and authority?

This is an important question, which cannot merely be brushed aside by reference to all the other restrictions on national independence accepted by successive British governments during this century. It may be true that the Common Market debate is not raising any new issue and that the treaties, the alliances, the international agreements and the international institutions already accepted by the British Government have so fettered their authority and independence – to a degree inconceivable to Sir Edward Grey or his predecessors – that the only remaining choice is between one kind of dependence and another. It has even been argued that the British Government might have more freedom of action – because of the consequent strengthening of the British economy – inside the Common Market than outside. But the original question stands. If the national interest centres on the independence and authority of the nation-state, why have so many British governments accepted such multifarious and far-reaching restrictions on both?

The usual answer is that, in the altered power ratios of the modern world, Britain's national capacity and economic resources are insufficient to permit her survival without a network of arrangements for mutual defence and co-operation. But, if two million Israelis can maintain complete independence in defiance of sixty million hostile neighbours, why cannot the far greater riches and far more numerous population of Britain be mobilized with corresponding success? How can Switzerland enjoy both peace and prosperity while scorning even membership of the United Nations as an unacceptable infringement of her sovereignty? It is not impossible to sketch on paper the steps whereby a British Government could recover their freedom of action – the expansion of agricultural production, the substitution of indigenous or synthetic materials for those now imported, the reduction of population, the mobilization of manpower and resources for national ends. Politicians evidently regard such slogans as 'Britain strong and free' as compatible with national aspirations and are accustomed to denounce British dependence on the United States or membership of the North Atlantic Treaty Organization. Why has none of them ever advocated a practical programme to give the Right strength and freedom and to withdraw the skirts of the Left from alien contamination? Why has the euphemistic concept of 'interdependence' been so easily and so generally accepted as 'in the national interest'?

These are anomalies which can only be explained by further modification of the tentative approaches so far made to a definition of the national interest. The first idea – that this corresponded to the material interests of the ruling class – failed to survive the test of 1939 and the war that followed. The second idea – that the national interest is centred in the maintenance of national independence and authority – is progressively harder to sustain from 1945 onwards and is particularly inadequate in the Common Market debate. But, if we take an offshoot of the first idea – preservation of the existing social order – and combine this with the second, we may reach a more viable definition:

the national interest is to maintain, to the extent compatible with preservation of the existing social order, the independence and authority of the nation-state.

Before proceeding to test this definition against the historical record, two important qualifications must be emphasized. The first is that the national interest is not the sole factor determining policy. It always has to be weighed against national aspirations and national capacities, either of which may inhibit or modify the course of action apparently dictated by the national interest. The second is that the three objectives embodied in this definition are variable, both in themselves and in relation to one another. Throughout British history there have been considerable fluctuations in the degree of independence, authority and social stability at which British governments have aimed and, when these objectives conflicted, in the relative importance attached to each. What seemed 'right', natural, inevitable to one century has appeared absurd to another. All that is claimed is that, in all its varying manifestations, the idea of the national interest has always embodied each of these three objectives and that, although one may temporarily predominate or be sacrificed, none has ever been wholly abandoned.

For instance, if we start in the tradition of the Whig historians at 1688, that was the year in which the British ruling class, rather than allow King James II to overturn the social order, temporarily sacrificed some of the independence of the nation-state by inviting foreign troops to install an alien monarch and subordinate British foreign policy to the needs of the Netherlands. Yet this expedient so reinforced the authority (greatly enfeebled under the Stuarts) of the nation-state that Walpole was later able to make his celebrated declaration of independence to another alien monarch anxious to embroil Britain in continental quarrels:

'Madam, there are fifty thousand men slain this year in

Europe, and not one Englishman, and besides the satisfaction it is to one's good nature to make this reflection, considering they owe their safety and their lives to those under whose care and protection they are, sure, in point of policy, too, it is no immaterial circumstance to be able to say that, whilst all the rest of Europe has paid their share to this diminution of their common strength, England remains in its full and unimpaired vigour.'[1]

In the language of the time Sir Robert Walpole was thus reconciling national aspirations and national interests and, although this particular passage refers only to the components of independence and authority, the preservation of the social order was never far from his thoughts. On another occasion he agreed with Lord Hervey that no argument constituted a more effective deterrent to the King's desire for British intervention in the European conflict than the risk this would entail to the maintenance of the Hanoverian dynasty and the social order this implied for Britain: 'the shadow of the Pretender will beat the whole Germanic body'.[2]

This was the beginning of a long period of British history in which the three objectives of independence, authority and social stability worked harmoniously together to form a conception of the national interest which, though its practical application led to diverse policies, scarcely varied in principle before the First World War. In 1793, for instance, the emergence of revolutionary France was as much a threat to the social order of Britain as to her national independence and authority, so that diplomatic and military manœuvres abroad were accompanied by measures of repression at home. What seems, in retrospect, the first fissure in this monolithic conception of the national interest came immediately before the First World War, when a section of the ruling class, anxious to

[1] Sir Robert Walpole was speaking to Queen Caroline for the ear of King George II, *Lord Hervey's Memoirs*, ed. Romney Sedgwick (William Kimber 1952).

[2] Op. cit., Chapter III.

preserve the existing social order in Ireland, challenged the authority of the nation-state, while others, for the first time in a century, showed signs of readiness to enlist the aid of foreign governments in the settlement of an internal dispute. This nascent conflict was quickly resolved by the outbreak of war with Germany, in which the independence and authority of the nation-state again became the paramount objectives. It was only after this war, partly because of the damage it did to the national capacity, partly because it sowed the seeds of social change and partly because it altered the character of national aspirations, that a situation emerged in which it came to appear that the three objectives of independence, authority and social stability might no longer be fully compatible, at least to the same extent as in the preceding two centuries.

This was nothing new. Under Tudors and Stuarts alike, the constant interaction of foreign and domestic affairs had been a familiar phenomenon and no British statesman of those periods would have considered it possible to regard foreign policy as a thing apart or the national interest as a conception independent of domestic politics. It was the century of peace and power between 1815 and 1914, in which Britain had seemed free to occupy herself with her own affairs without regard to their possible repercussions on her unchallenged independence and external authority, that had created this illusion and conferred upon the idea of the national interest such a spuriously uncontroversial character.

The true test of this three-pronged definition of the national interest must thus be sought in more recent history, when conditions in Britain and her place in the world bear closer comparison with those of today. Before 1939 successive British governments showed, as some of their opponents argued at the time and as events later demonstrated, insufficient concern for the independence and authority of the nation-state. It is at least plausible that, whether in the economic decisions of 1931 or in the diplomatic and military decisions of later years, they and the British ruling class were primarily concerned to preserve the existing social order. Indeed, when the events of 1939 forced an abrupt reversal of foreign policy, this led to one of the most rapid and drastic periods of social change in British history, culminating in the establishment of what was virtually a new social order and a much altered ruling class. This does not impair the validity of social stability as a component in the national interest. On the contrary, once the dust had settled, it was obvious that a much larger section of the population had now acquired a vested interest in the – new – existing order of society. Social security, the National Health Service, full employment were now part of the existing social order and their preservation became an element of the national interest. It was this new social structure that was now incompatible with heroic theories of national mobilization for military and economic self-sufficiency. Even if national aspirations had permitted the retention of the British Empire – and we have noted in the previous chapter the force of negative tendencies in this field – the altered conception of the national interest imposed by a new social structure made this impossible. The authority of the British nation-state, on which even in 1939 the sun had never set, had to be contracted accordingly.

Contracted – but not abolished. One of the characteristics of post-war foreign policy has been the effort towards all three of the objectives set forth as components of the national interest. Immediately after the war, for instance, when a new social structure largely evolved under wartime pressures was being given institutional shape, this seemed to be the dominant factor. To sustain it sacrifices were necessary, not only of the external authority of the nation-state, but also of its independence. The American Loan of 1945[1] inaugurated a tradition of accepting

[1] There were earlier precedents, but these were regarded as exceptional expedients in time of emergency.

restrictions on British policy as the price of financial assistance. This was a deliberate choice and the arguments put forward in 1945 and 1946 show that the advantages of accepting the loan were anxiously weighed against the sacrifice of independent authority this would entail. Politically, at least, it might even have been easier to make a different choice in 1945 than on subsequent occasions. The Welfare State had not then been established, nor had the austerities of wartime been appreciably relaxed. It is thus arguable that the existing social order could have been preserved without the American Loan and that the national aspiration for social justice and an improved standard of living played a greater part in the decision than the national interest, at least as this has been defined here. This is a debatable and somewhat academic point. But, once the decision was taken and the transformation of British society had actually begun, the new standards thus created became needs rather than aspirations and modified the national interest accordingly.

Thereafter, as each successive economic crisis confronted the British Government of the day, no major reduction in the advantages conferred by the Welfare State could be regarded as compatible with preservation of existing social order. This does not mean that successive governments were bound, in the national interest, to sacrifice a degree of independence in order to secure financial assistance. These economic crises might perhaps have been surmounted by an accelerated transfer of sovereignty in British dependencies and by a correspondingly rapid reduction in British forces and British expenditure overseas. In practice, however, successive British governments, while contracting their authority in some parts of the world, went to great lengths to maintain it in others. Costly military operations were conducted in Palestine, in Malaya, in Kenya, in Cyprus and in Borneo during the two decades between 1946 and 1966. Military bases were expensively improved, and military stores accumulated, in the Suez Canal Zone, in Cyprus, in Aden, in Singapore and in the Persian Gulf. Even where overseas military expenditure was ostensibly incurred as a long-term contribution to the preservation of British independence – by participation in the Korean War or by keeping British forces in Germany throughout this period – this was also regarded as maintaining British external authority in the form of British influence on the policies of the United States and German governments.

It was the economic burden of this constant effort to maintain external authority, quite as much as the need to preserve the existing social order, that demanded the acceptance of financial assistance on terms derogatory to the independence of the nation-state. Nor was this independence sacrificed in the financial sphere alone. The deployment of British forces overseas reduced the manpower and the resources available for the defence of Britain itself. American bases were set up in Britain and manned by American forces under the control of the United States Government. Their presence helped to protect British independence against any threat from a third party, but at the price of dependence on American goodwill. Even British forces were equipped with American weapons to be used only at the discretion of the United States Government.

Yet even these unprecedented sacrifices did not imply that the objective of independence had been wholly displaced from the national interest by those of authority or the social order. It was rather that the experience of the Second World War, reinforced immediately afterwards by realization of the alarming strength and hostility of the Soviet Union, had persuaded, perhaps temporarily, successive British governments that the independence of the nation-state could be preserved only in diminished form. Their underlying attachment to independence persisted and its influence may frequently be detected in policies or decisions – the development and maintenance of the British nuclear deterrent, Lord Avon's attitude at the 1954 Geneva Conference on Indo-China, the regular pilgrimage to Moscow of British Prime Ministers – that seemed primarily to assert Britain's continued ability to differ from the United States.

Indeed, the more closely one examines the confusing record of British foreign policy since the war, the harder it becomes to explain its inconsistencies and changes of direction except in terms of a conception of the national interest embodying distinct and sometimes incompatible objectives. This emerges most clearly from British policy towards Europe. In the years immediately following the war the maintenance of British authority and independence against the potential Russian menace seemed to require closer association with Europe and the British Government of the day went further in this direction than had, perhaps, ever before been attempted in time of peace with the Treaties of Dunkirk and of Brussels, the North Atlantic Treaty and the Organization for European Economic Co-operation. During this period, too, there was even some British encouragement for the idea of European unity. Yet, as this idea began to gather strength and to find concrete expression in a series of institutions, whether achieved or projected, each of which demanded from its members a degree of limitation on national sovereignty, the British attitude altered. The European Coal and Steel Community, the European Defence Community, the European Economic Community, these and other arrangements were each judged incompatible with national independence. Only when a series of economic crises had made it obvious that preservation of the social order required some sacrifice, whether of independence or of authority or even of both, were successive British governments driven, just as Chamberlain had been driven, to reverse their policies and to seek, against far greater foreign opposition and on much worse terms, a solution previously rejected as incompatible with the national interest.

It may thus be argued that this definition passes the preliminary tests: it is consistent with the policies actually followed by British governments and helps to explain their vagaries; it meets the obvious needs of the ruling class, yet is not incompatible with those of the rest of the people. There remain, however, two questions to be answered concerning its validity before any attempt is made to examine its utility: has anything superfluous been included and has anything essential been left out?

In this connexion it is perhaps unnecessary to consider objections to the idea of a nation-state. Whether or not the inhabitants of East Anglia would be better off if their region constituted one province of a united Europe in which Britain no longer existed as a distinct political entity, this is not an issue at all likely to become actual during the currency of this book. Moreover, unless the existence of the nation-state can be assumed, there is no national interest and no foreign policy and no need for the present work. Granted the existence of the nation-state, however, it is necessary to distinguish between the objectives of independence and of authority and to explain precisely what is meant by each.

In some circumstances, of course, independence and authority are obverse and reverse of the same coin. Whenever the British Government have failed to maintain their internal authority, some degree of risk has arisen to the independence of the nation-state, but this is not a problem which has been of much importance since the seventeenth century, though there was at least a hint of it at the time of the naval mutinies of 1797 and in the pre-1914 preparations for civil war in Ireland. As a general rule, however, there is a clear distinction. Independence is essentially the ability of the nation-state to disregard foreign views in ordering its own affairs;

authority (so far as foreign policy is concerned) is the ability to influence events and decisions overseas. These do not necessarily go hand in hand. For many years after 1945 Sweden and Switzerland enjoyed greater independence than Britain: they had no allies to consult, no Commonwealth to appease, no foreign creditors to placate. But they exercised less external authority. There were no overseas territories under their control, no garrisons or warships in distant parts of the world, no disposable power or resulting prestige to reinforce the arguments of their Ambassadors.

Britain, on the other hand, often derived increased authority from the very factors that curtailed her independence. The existence of the sterling area imposed crippling restrictions on her domestic policies, but gave her greater influence in matters of international finance than her actual resources or dwindling reputation for financial expertise might otherwise have commanded. The alliances that distorted Britain's economy and fettered her independence also enabled her to intervene, without risk to the security of her own islands, in distant parts of the world.

The case for the independence of the nation-state, which offers the British people the maximum opportunity of being governed in accordance with their particular requirements, may nevertheless seem more obvious than the case for its external authority. If national aspirations are excluded from the argument, on what rational grounds does Britain require to exercise authority beyond her territorial limits and to what extent?

This difficult question has been intermittently debated and variously answered ever since the accession to the English throne of William of Normandy gave the nation-state its first heady whiff of external authority. Historically there seem to have been three main incentives to its exercise: to provide the State with an additional source of revenue; to facilitate the conduct of military operations;

and to protect the private interests of British subjects. The first is largely obsolete – even the taxes which provoked the American revolution would have met only a fraction of the British Government's expenditure in the American colonies – and the exercise of external authority has long represented a net liability to the British Exchequer (though not necessarily to the national economy). The second is not strictly relevant, because the purpose of the military operations that would be facilitated by the maintenance of external authority was generally that of maintaining external authority, but some of the exceptions to this circular argument will be considered subsequently. Only the third of these incentives, the most important today and also subject to much the same advantages and drawbacks as the other two, will be examined in any detail in the present chapter.

From the earliest times enterprising citizens have ventured abroad, whether in person or through the investment of their capital, in search of profit. Their activities frequently aroused foreign opposition, sometimes in the absence of effective foreign authority, sometimes because that authority was hostile. To withstand this opposition the merchant venturers sought the protection of their own nation-state. When this was granted, the State normally had two motives, one economic, the other political.

The economic motive was that the profits brought back to Britain by these private individuals – or the imports they facilitated – were of advantage to the nation-state as a whole. Even in Tudor times, when English imports were mainly of luxuries, the profits earned by trade were of importance to the economy and, above all, to the ruling class, who were naturally also the principal consumers of the imported luxuries. As trade increased, these profits became essential to the preservation of the social order and, during the nineteenth century, the British people grew to depend for their very existence on imported food and raw materials. As the cost of these imports was seldom fully covered by exports, the repatriation of profits from abroad thus became important to the people as a whole, even if the principal beneficiaries were still the ruling class, whose predominant role in the determination of the national interest has already been noted.

The political motive is expressed in the ancient legal maxim: protection draws allegiance and allegiance draws protection. To retain the allegiance of its nationals overseas the State had to afford them protection. This was particularly important in times when the precarious authority of the State could be jeopardized by even small-scale defections. Nowadays a transfer of allegiance by an overseas community can seldom threaten the security of the nation-state in Britain itself, but it can still entail the loss of important political and commercial advantages. As long as British expatriates retain their allegiance, they usually employ their local influence to the benefit of Britain. It is not only their own profits and purchases which are directed to Britain, but also those of the foreigners among whom they reside; not only in matters of commerce that their efforts and their influence are employed to British advantage. Naturally this loyalty is not entirely prompted by interest – sentiment also plays its part. But no sentiment is politically so efficacious as patriotism and this seldom survives a transfer of allegiance. Even Scotland, who commands the sentimental attachment of her expatriates for generations after their departure from her borders, seldom derives much material advantage from those who have renounced their British nationality. And the proportion of British expatriates who forsake their allegiance to become the naturalized citizens of a foreign State is always highest in those countries (such as the United States) where the expatriate no longer relies on British protection.

This link between allegiance and protection applies to communities as well as to individuals. The loyalty to

Britain of the English-speaking countries of the Commonwealth has been directly proportional to their reliance on British protection. As this has declined, so has the proportionate importance of British trade and investment in these countries and so, sentiment notwithstanding, has their readiness to afford political or military assistance. In the Suez Crisis of 1956 only Australia and New Zealand gave unquestioning support, but, by 1963, this had been transferred to the United States in Vietnam rather than to Britain in Borneo. This trend will probably be accelerated by Britain's proclaimed intention of withdrawing her military forces from the Far East. The predominant rôle of interest, as opposed to sentiment, is further illustrated by the fervent loyalty to Britain, during recent years, of the people of Gibraltar. They mostly lack the common ancestry and traditions which were once supposed to guarantee the continued attachment to Britain of Australia and New Zealand, but the Gibraltarians still rely on British protection.

The material advantages of maintaining British external authority need to be emphasized, because argument on this issue is so often distorted by appeals to sentiment and tradition. The sentimental invocation of Britain's rôle in the world can irritate realists into overlooking the practical benefits of external authority; parrot-cries of imperialism may exasperate them into forgetting its cost. Yet, in terms of the national interest, these are the essential arguments which have confronted British governments throughout the centuries. In Tudor times, for instance, it was considered important for England to hold a port across the Channel as a secure trading-post for her merchants. In the eyes of later governments the advantages of this expedient were outweighed by the expense and inconvenience of maintaining it against the growing authority of the nation-states of Europe, particularly as these States became increasingly disposed to tolerate and even to protect British trade and British merchants. But the same expedient was again adopted in the Americas, in Asia and in Africa, as long as the need for protection existed and could be met without efforts and expense disproportionate to the benefits obtained.

Weighing the cost of external authority against its advantages has never been easy, because both sides of the equation are affected by multipliers of a somewhat indeterminate character. Who could reasonably have been expected to foresee that the acquisition of a few fortified trading-posts in India would gradually involve Britain, step by often reluctant step, in extending her authority to the entire sub-continent, or that this authority would then have to be buttressed by a whole chain of intermediate bases and possessions, by European alliances to help secure those possessions and, to maintain these alliances, by two World Wars of which the expense finally induced Britain to relinquish her authority in India? If the cost of maintaining a particular element of British external authority is liable to unpredictable expansion, so are its advantages. The beginning and the end of British rule in India may have involved disproportionate costs, but, for the many years in the middle period, it provided a self-sustaining reinforcement of British external authority, which was upheld in China and in the Persian Gulf by Indian troops financed from Indian revenue. There was also another multiplier – to be considered more fully in a later chapter – that of prestige. Every instance in which Britain's external authority was successfully upheld in the face of opposition made the next challenge easier to resist and less likely even to occur. At its zenith the British Empire was maintained with far less effort and expenditure than in its growth or its decline.

These considerations again illustrate the dangers of the pragmatic fallacy: the idea that every problem can be judged on its own merits. Any attempt to assess the cost-effectiveness of maintaining a particular element of Britain's external authority must take account of the wider repercussions that any decision will entail. To hold a base may involve the conquest of its hinterland; to abandon it may invite a threat to another. This is why external authority has been treated as an intrinsic component of the national interest and not merely, as other writers have preferred, as a derivative of national security or of the national interest in freedom of trade and navigation. These considerations may have prompted the acquisition of external authority and justified its maintenance. They can legitimately be invoked in considering its practical application or modification. But nine centuries have not merely encrusted the idea of external authority with sentiment and tradition: they have transformed it from a mere expedient to an objective in its own right. History suggests that, when British external authority is at its height, the world offers greater advantages to the British people, particularly but not exclusively, to the ruling class, than when this authority reaches such a nadir as that of the later seventeenth century. This may not necessarily be true in the future and the advantages of external authority must, in any case, be weighed against other components of the national interest as well as against national aspirations and capacities. On the whole, however, it may be argued that external authority, as a component of the national interest, is more comprehensive and, historically, perhaps more potent and enduring, than those considerations arising from the balance of payments with which it is so closely associated. Theoretically it is the most debatable element of the national interest, but in practice it seems to offer an easier and more acceptable test of policies and decisions than the admitted, though sometimes less specifically directional, interest in freedom of trade and navigation. It would be difficult, in the light of the historical record, to substitute these, or other words of a commercial character, for the term 'authority', in advancing the proposition that the national interest requires the maintenance, to the extent compatible with preservation of the social order and of national independence, of the nation-state.

To many readers, however, external authority may seem a less objectionable component of the national interest than preservation of the existing social order. Even if this can be deduced from the actions of successive governments and attributed to the needs of the ruling class, ought it to constitute a major component of the national interest in preference to such more attractive ideas as peace, prosperity, progress, security or even, in the unique and splendid words of the American Declaration of Independence, 'life, liberty and the pursuit of happiness'? It ought not, perhaps, but it does. The historical record shows that British governments have far more frequently been prepared to abandon any or all of these desirable objectives than they have to risk the social order. Indeed, the national interest is seldom more earnestly invoked than as a prelude to demands for sacrifice, often explicitly in order to 'preserve our way of life'.

It is unnecessary, in a work devoted to foreign policy, to emulate any of the eminent persons who have attempted, generally in terms more remarkable for eloquence than for precision or uniformity, to define this way of life. One tentative comment may, however, be ventured. In emergency neither individuals nor nations can hope to preserve all their possessions; they save what they can or what they most value. In the supreme emergency of the Second World War Britain abandoned General Elections, Habeas Corpus, the freedom of the Press and many of the rights and liberties of the individual. Food was rationed and men and women were compelled, by conscription, to risk their lives. The social order, whether this was reflected in the privileges of trade unionists or in those of the Brigade of Guards, survived relatively unscathed. Perhaps this was mere coincidence, perhaps there was nothing in the social order detrimental to the war effort, but it is just conceivable that the British are readier to sacrifice their lives, their liberties and their food, than they are that intricate honeycomb of painfully acquired privileges, of relative rights, of status, that, at any given moment, constitutes the social order. This does not mean that the social order is immutable. On the contrary, it is in constant evolution. It is simply that its preservation, whatever its contemporary nature, seems always to have contributed an element to the national interest more equivalent in force to the objectives of independence and authority than principles, or even concrete aspirations, of apparently greater value. The then Chancellor of the Exchequer gave this notion a neat expression when the House of Commons were trying to decide which sacrifices would be least damaging to the national interest, all three aspects of which were invoked by various speakers. He said: 'One must surely distinguish between the postponement of a most desirable advance and going back on what already exists.'[1]

'What already exists', indeed, is fundamental to the entire concept of the national interest in Britain and it influences contemporary judgements in respect of independence and of external authority no less than in regard to the social order. In the eighteenth and nineteenth centuries the importance thus attached to the *status quo* was not only natural, but relatively harmless. The three components of the national interest altered only slowly, whether in themselves or in their relation to one another. Men whose ideas had been formed in their twenties or thirties seldom needed to adjust them drastically on reaching a position of power or influence in their fifties or sixties. The problems might be new, but they existed within a familiar frame of reference. Today this frame is fluid and British policy in the third quarter of the twentieth century more ephemeral than at any time since the seventeenth century. What exists today no longer reliably suggests what should be done tomorrow.

[1] Mr. Jenkins, *Hansard*, 17 January 1968.

With the present yielding beneath our uncertain feet, it is natural to look to the past for some reflected ray of light. Mere precedent, however, will not do: no event, no combination of circumstance, no problem is ever precisely reproduced. History must first be interpreted by theory, so as to disentangle from the jumble of vanished problems and forgotten decisions those few significant strands of purpose or success that might still offer usable clues in the contemporary labyrinth. Any such theory is necessarily arbitrary: we find what we look for and our interpretation of the past is coloured by the preoccupation of the present. This is no bad thing when the object is contemporary relevance rather than historic truth. But the relevance must not be contemporary to the point of being as ephemeral as the policies it is intended to influence. Men of power read books, if at all, in the leisure of their youthful impotence. If, twenty years later, these books are entirely out of date, such influence as they may have exercised will be pernicious. There have been many such books.

An attempt has accordingly been made to define the enduring elements of the national interest in terms sufficiently general to have some chance of preserving their relevance for perhaps a generation. The weakness of this approach is that, in striving to eliminate the ephemeral, there may also be some impairment of immediately practical utility. Whether or not the definition of the national interest here advanced is correct, it has been argued as applicable no less to the past than to the present. But, in seeking the elements common to more than one century, there has inevitably been some loss of the precise and the specific. Does what still remains offer any practical assistance in the formation of policy and the taking of actual decisions?

One obvious test is suggested by a problem already frequently mentioned: President Nasser's nationalization of the Suez Canal Company on 26 July 1956. The definition of the national interest set out in this chapter should, if it is valid, help to explain why the British Government responded as they did to Nasser; if it is useful, it should also suggest a course of action less damaging than that actually adopted. Naturally neither the explanation nor the suggestion can be more than partial, for policy is determined by aspirations and capacities as well as by interests.

Nasser's announcement was seen by the British Government as likely to have three consequences: one actual and two potential. Firstly, nationalization of the Suez Canal Company would deprive the British Government of their 45 per cent of the profits expected during the twelve years then remaining of the Company's concession. Secondly, the passage of British shipping through the canal might be obstructed, whether deliberately or merely by incompetence, once the canal was under entirely Egyptian management and control. Finally, this act of expropriation, having been expressly proclaimed as a gesture of defiance by Arab nationalism against imperialism, might be imitated by other Arab countries with important British assets within their boundaries. The accuracy of these predictions – and the material repercussions on the British economy – were the subject of much argument at the time, but this aspect was obviously less important to the British Government than a fourth factor. By taking a step with such obvious potential repercussions and by the language employed in its justification, Nasser had deliberately defied the authority in the Middle East of the British nation-state.

This authority had once been real. For over seventy years Egypt had been garrisoned by British troops and had intermittently provided a base for the British Mediterranean Fleet. These forces had not only made the Suez Canal a safe highway for British shipping and, as necessary, denied it to the ships of hostile nations: they had enabled British advisers and ambassadors to dictate the composition and policy of Egyptian governments. The reserve of strength furnished by these forces, together with the ability of the Indian Army to intervene in Iraq, Iran or the Persian Gulf, had also enabled a handful of British advisers and officers, occasionally assisted by small numbers of soldiers or aircraft, to exert a decisive influence in other Middle Eastern countries as well. With the solitary exception of Aden no Middle Eastern territory had ever formed part of the British Empire, yet none had failed, at one time or another, in greater or lesser degree, to acknowledge the force of British authority. As a result British enterprise throughout the region had enjoyed effective protection; trade had flourished; vast oil fields had been discovered and exploited; profits had flowed with the oil to Britain and the Suez Canal had become one of the main arteries of British commerce. That the national interest required the maintenance of an authority which had brought such advantages might well have seemed a self-evident proposition.

It might, that is, in 1945, when the strategic requirements of the Second World War had, perhaps inadvertently, brought this authority to its brief zenith, with British forces in almost every country of the Middle East and with the governments of the region either under actual British control or responsive to British influence. Whether this extensive and solid authority could or should have been retained is irrelevant to the present argument: well before 1956 it had, in fact, been relinquished. The process began with the loss in 1947 of the western and eastern buttresses – the British garrison in Cairo and the availability of the Indian Army. It ended in 1954, when withdrawal from the Canal Zone removed the last effective British force[1] in the heart of the Middle East, leaving only detachments (often already pre-empted) on the periphery; the small garrison of Aden, some troops on

[1] The 10th Hussars in Jordan were intended as a deterrent to an attack by Israel, not to assert authority in Jordan, for which task they were inadequate.

the wrong side of the Western Desert, rather more troops embattled in Cyprus and the scattered warships that patrolled the surrounding seas.

In 1956 British authority in the Middle East no longer existed. It had been replaced by British influence, a lath and plaster structure of reluctantly accepted treaties, of paper promises, of unsupported advisers, the whole precariously sustained by tradition, by a dwindling prestige, by the interests of a few local rulers. Repeated shocks – the seizure of the Abadan refinery in 1951, for instance – had cracked, but not demolished this façade, for the limited character of each British response could always be attributed to cunning as well as to weakness. Iran, for instance, had gained nothing by her seizure of Abadan until, years later, she had to reach agreement with the British. To the older generation of Arabs it still seemed that the lion might not be dead, but only sleeping. The young men, less blinded by their memories, had fewer doubts.

Without this mist of romantic recollection, the choice should have been equally clear in London. By 1956 there could no longer be any question of maintaining British authority in the Middle East. This had already been relinquished, not least by Lord Avon himself in 1954. The options now open to the British Government were, on the one hand, another patched-up compromise of the Abadan pattern whereby, with some degree of international assistance, British face might be partially saved at the expense of material concessions, or, on the other hand, a major effort to reassert, in conditions far less favourable than those of 1882, a now vanished British authority. It is ironical that Lord Avon should have been so strongly influenced in his actual decision by his resolve to avoid the errors of Chamberlain: in fact the adventure of 1956 imitated that of 1939. The years of appeasement, of concession, of retreat were suddenly reversed by a desperate bid for the reassertion of authority. This is a recurrent pattern in British history – the belated realization of the pitfalls of pragmatism. But Chamberlain at least understood that his change of course would entail a major war if it was to be successful.

The Suez episode also helps to justify the insistence on the maintenance of authority rather than the protection of specific British assets or the preservation of the freedom of trade and navigation, as the essential component of the national interest. There were, after all, substantial Egyptian assets in Britain that could have been used to enforce the payment of compensation for the nationalization of the Company. There was an obvious Egyptian interest in maintaining international traffic through the canal and there was an equally obvious Arab interest in the continued sale of oil. This coincidence of interests admittedly provided a less solid guarantee than British authority, but had been found sufficient in other parts of the world. The question posed in 1956 did not really turn on the money Britain might lose by the nationalization of the Company, or on transit through the Canal or on the future of British dividends and oil supplies from the Middle East. All these were less jeopardized by President Nasser's action than by Lord Avon's response. The true issue was: who should have authority in Egypt and by extension in the Middle East – the British Government or the Egyptian? If this had been an open question, if the answer had depended on the free choice, the mere preference, of the British Government, there can be no doubt as to the requirements of the national interest. British authority is, by definition, better than foreign authority and, in an ideal world, would no doubt be universal. As things actually are, the maintenance of existing British authority may reasonably be regarded as being, other factors permitting, in the national interest, but its extension is necessarily subject to severer limitations. The relevance to the Suez Crisis of 1956 of the national interest, as here defined, is this: the British Government were right to believe that the national interest required them to maintain the authority of the nation-state; they were wrong in thinking that this still existed in the Middle East, or, if they realized that it had already been relinquished, in thinking that national capacities and national aspirations would permit its restoration. The national interest is a major factor in the formation of policy, but it is neither simple nor monolithic nor susceptible of instinctive perception. Its various components must be separately considered in relation to the objective facts of every situation and the purpose thus indicated must then be weighed against the national aspirations already touched on and the national capacities which are to be the subject of the following chapters. Interest may never lie, but it may be misinterpreted and it is not self-sufficient.

4

NATIONAL CAPACITIES: DIPLOMATIC AND ECONOMIC

'Nous avons plus de force que de volonté, et c'est souvent pour nous excuser à nous-mêmes *que nous nous imaginons* que les choses sont impossibles.'

La Rochefoucauld[1]

CAPACITY, according to the dictionary,[2] is the power of holding or grasping, a suggestive definition when foreign policy is in question, but one that needs to be amplified and explained before it can be applied to the concept of national capacities. So far this term has been loosely employed to describe the resources available to the State for the attainment of its objectives in foreign policy, the assumption being that aspirations and interests combine to provide the motive, whereas capacities furnish the means. It has also been suggested that the assessment of national capacities plays a part in shaping policy as well as in its execution. In choosing their course of action governments usually consider not only what is desirable, but also what is possible, so that a choice indicated by the combined influence of aspirations and interests may be excluded or modified because it fails to correspond to national capacities. These thus constitute a limiting factor in the formation of policy.

This view of national capacities as a purely negative influence on policy is not universally accepted. The idea

[1] François VI, duc de La Rochefoucauld *Maximes*, Ed. F. C. Green (Cambridge University Press 1945).

[2] *Collins' New English Dictionary*.

has often been advanced that the nature and extent of a nation's resources can exert a positive influence and even provide a motive for policy. Theories of this kind go far beyond the obvious repercussions on foreign policy of the need to import commodities not available in Britain and to pay for them by exports. It has already been argued that the protection of foreign trade sometimes demanded the exercise of external authority. British merchants, for instance, could only hope to profit from the sale abroad of British woollen cloth if they could be reasonably sure that nobody would rob them of the cloth before they had sold it or of the proceeds before these could be repatriated. At certain periods and in certain countries this assurance could only be provided by their own nation-state, which had to extend its authority accordingly. The quest for exotic products and for profit beyond the seas has exercised a potent influence on British foreign policy throughout the centuries, but no addition to earlier arguments is needed to explain why the British people once wanted spices to season their salt meat and now desire petrol to drive their cars. In each case the preservation of the social order could be held to require the exercise of an external authority varying with the circumstances of the time. The challenge to the line of argument so far employed occurs only when it is asserted that British foreign policy was not determined by the needs and wants of the British people, but by the automatic operation of a particular economic system: that external authority was not exerted to remedy economic deficiencies but to relieve the pressure of surplus economic capacities.

Ideas of this kind range from the simple observation that a higher rate of return on capital may sometimes be achieved by employing it overseas to the elaborate Marxist theory of imperialism,[1] but most of them have certain features in common. They do not assign the motives of

[1] See Kemp, *Theories of Imperialism* (Dennis Dobson 1967) for a lucid exposition.

foreign policy to the mere existence of economic resources[1] – the volume of British steel production, for instance – but to the operation of various kinds of economic system. Marxists, for instance, argue that imperialism results from the inescapable need of capitalism to realize surplus values. The explanations offered by the economists are thus no less theoretical than those suggested in this book and, because each is based on particular assumptions about the nature of economic structures and their influence on human decisions, each is essentially a political theory. Fortunately there is no need to examine any of these conflicting, complex and controversial arguments because of another feature common to most of them: their avowedly cosmopolitan character and their express limitation to particular phases of economic development. The Marxists, for instance, are concerned with tendencies inherent in capitalism as a whole and do not profess to explain the differences between the foreign policies of Great Britain and of Sweden or the affinities between Russian foreign policy under capitalism and under communism. Indeed, they reject the validity of individual decisions, or even relationships extending over years between one State and another, as tests of their theories. Nor would they regard the exertion of English authority in North America during the seventeenth century as at all comparable with similar phenomena in the different economic circumstances of later centuries. Although economic theories, in common with those of anthropology, psychology or zoology, may assist in plumbing the ultimate springs of human motives, they are less immediately relevant to the international decisions of British governments than the more limited concepts of the authority, the independence and the social order of the nation-state. Therefore, although economic factors will

[1] The supposed propensity of armaments, by their mere existence, to encourage wars in which they might be employed seems an exception, but this is really a political theory depending on assumptions about soldiers.

occasionally be considered as providing a particular incentive to individual decisions, the general assumption will be that economic capacities constitute one of the means of foreign policy rather than its end or motive force.

Foreign policy, it was earlier suggested, is mainly concerned with disputes and it is in relation to disputes that the assessment of national capacities is most important. This is a problem to which several approaches are possible. If a dispute already exists, the British Government must consider what pressures are most likely to induce the foreign government concerned to give way, what resources are available for the application of such pressures, whether the use of these resources would conflict with other objectives and whether the cost of employing them would be in proportion to the value of the result to be achieved. It is in this form that the need to assess national capacities most frequently arises in practice and, although the questions posed involve such difficult and uncertain factors as the reactions to be expected from foreign governments, this is nevertheless the easiest kind of problem encountered in relation to national capacities, because it is concerned with what already exists. When a dispute has actually begun, the number of unknown quantities is greatly reduced. When Lord Palmerston made Don Pacifico's claim for compensation a cause of dispute with the Greek Government, he decided to apply pressure by imposing a naval blockade of Greece and by the seizure of Greek shipping. He knew the extent of British naval resources and was able to estimate – accurately, as it turned out – the likely reactions of the Greek Government and of their potential allies, France and Russia. It was thus relatively easy for him to decide that Britain possessed the national capacity to enforce the payment by the Greek Government of compensation for the alleged damage to Don Pacifico's property during a riot. He acted accordingly and was entirely successful, though the measures he adopted were much criticized at the time as disproportionate to his objective.

Much more difficult problems arise when the disputes are only potential and it is a question, not of assessing the adequacy of existing resources to meet a specific requirement, but of trying to ensure that policy and capacities will be compatible in contingencies that can only be guessed at. The most obvious example is the relationship that ought to exist between foreign policy and defence policy. Ideally a British Government should either adopt a foreign policy calculated to avoid disputes beyond the capacity of the armed forces to determine or else raise the capacity of these forces to match the level of the disputes likely to be engendered by the foreign policy actually adopted. In practice most British governments have underestimated the provocative character of their foreign policy and overestimated the effectiveness of their armed forces. Even during the nineteenth century, when the predominance of the Royal Navy encouraged successive British governments to follow policies chosen without much regard for the susceptibilities of other nations, disputes often arose in which the British Government were obliged to give way for lack of a strong enough army. In 1853, for instance, Canada's vulnerability to invasion deterred the British Government from more than a protest against American naval bombardment of Greytown in the British Central American protectorate of the Mosquito Coast, an act described by the British Foreign Secretary as an outrage 'without a parallel in the annals of modern times'.[1]

This was, perhaps, not the easiest of disputes to foresee and it would be unreasonable to expect the British Government to be capable of preventing, or successfully terminating, every dispute which the malice or folly of foreign governments might thrust upon them. But, when

[1] Lord Strang, *Britain in World Affairs*, Chapter IX (Faber & Faber 1961).

the British Government themselves take the initiative, whether by starting an actual dispute or by embarking upon a course of action likely to lead to dispute, common sense requires that they should first decide whether sufficient national capacities are available for such disputes to be carried to an advantageous conclusion. This is always a difficult question to answer correctly, because it necessarily involves a guess at the nature and extent of the opposition to be expected from the foreign government concerned and, the more remote is the potential dispute, the more uncertain this guess is likely to be. This makes it all the more important that policies should constantly be reassessed in the light both of national capacities and of the type of pressures these capacities might be expected to sustain. In 1957, for instance, the then British Government made the following declaration of policy in connexion with the perennial dispute between Israel and the Arab States:

> 'The Straits of Tiran must be regarded as an international waterway, through which the vessels of all nations have a right of passage. Her Majesty's Government will assert this right on behalf of all British shipping and they are prepared to join with others to secure general recognition of this right.'[1]

Ten years later, after an announcement of the Egyptian Government's intention to close the Straits of Tiran to Israeli ships and to the carriage of strategic goods to Israel, another British Government reaffirmed the 1957 declaration and were supported, in so doing, by the Leader of the Opposition.[1] In the course of the debate that followed, in which the Government's declaration received widespread support, Sir Alec Douglas-Home remarked that:

> 'It is right to make, or seek to get, a positive and firm declaration that the Gulf and the Straits will be kept open.'[1]

He went on:

[1] *Hansard*, 31 May 1967.

'It would not be reasonable, and I have no intention of doing so, to press the Prime Minister as to how the Gulf and the Straits should be kept open.'[1]

In the light of subsequent events, particularly the hostile Arab reactions and the resulting damage to British property and British interests in the Arab countries, the reader may wonder whether Sir Alec should not, after all, have pressed his question and whether there had, in fact, been an adequate reassessment of British national capacities in 1967 before the decision was reached to reaffirm the policy of 1957.

This particular doubt may not finally be resolved before the relevant archives are opened to inspection in 1997, but this need not prevent consideration meanwhile of the kind of assessment which, it is suggested, should precede the adoption by British governments of policies likely to involve the British nation-state in disputes. In doing so, the first step is to examine the nature of the expedients open to British governments and of the capacities on which these are based. There are four broad categories: diplomatic, economic, military and, though this enters into all the other three, moral.

The diplomatic category embraces every means of exerting influence by the use of words alone: public speeches, representations by Ambassadors, appeals to the United Nations, invoking alliances, seeking the assistance of third parties. It is treated as a national capacity, because its effectiveness depends on the size, geographical distribution and quality of the British diplomatic service, on the nature of British relations with other governments, on the British position as a permanent member of the United Nations Security Council, on the international reputation at any given time of the British Government and on a host of other factors independent of the nature or merits of any particular dispute. A foreign government, for instance, will often make a concession to British wishes merely be-

[1] *Hansard*, 31 May 1967.

cause of a desire to maintain friendly relations, or because a British ambassador has been able to employ timely and persuasive arguments or because of a desire to avoid embarrassing publicity.

If, therefore, a dispute arises, or is foreseen, with a foreign government, the first question to be considered is whether British diplomatic capacities are likely to be enough to avoid, to limit or to terminate the dispute. Obviously this will be more difficult in the case of a foreign government not amenable to British diplomatic influence. Albania, for instance, has no diplomatic relations with Britain and it would be hard to think of any third party at once willing and able to persuade the Albanian Government to meet British wishes in the event of dispute. Nor, during the last two decades, have the Albanian Government given much indication of responsiveness to publicity, to the decisions of international organizations or to other forms of verbal pressure. In the diplomatic field, therefore, British national capacities in relation to any dispute with Albania during this period might reasonably be assessed as nil.

There are other countries, however, with which British relations are so close and friendly, that most disputes are easily resolved or avoided by diplomatic methods. This is because both the British Government and the foreign government concerned normally take the view that the maintenance of these friendly relations is more important than any single cause of dispute. Thus, when a dispute arose between Britain and the other members of the European Free Trade Association concerning the British import surcharges of 1964, British diplomatic capacities proved sufficient to resolve it in a manner demanding concessions by both sides: temporary acceptance by the foreign governments concerned of these surcharges and their subsequent withdrawal by the British Government. In cases of this kind, British diplomatic capacity may be regarded as a fund of goodwill on which the British

Government may draw to obtain foreign concessions, but which must nevertheless be replenished by British policies welcome to the foreign governments concerned.

This is one case in which national capacities can exert a positive influence on policy. Where friendly relations exist with a foreign government, these constitute a British asset; something which can be employed for the advantageous resolution of future disputes. The Foreign Office and, above all, the British Embassy in the country concerned will be very conscious of the value of this asset. They will accordingly advocate policies specifically intended to preserve friendly relations, even if these do not directly promote British national interests and even if these policies involve British concessions in actual or potential disputes. In extreme cases this may even result in complaints that the interests of British subjects, national interests or national aspirations are being sacrificed to the maintenance of friendly relations without any adequate return in the shape of concessions by the foreign government concerned. Such criticism is often reciprocated. British Members of Parliament have frequently complained of the alleged subservience to the United States of successive British governments, but American Congressmen and Senators have just as often reproached their own Government for supine acquiescence in British policies supposedly inimical to the United States. Both sides may have an arguable case on the particular issues they select, because, for at least the last twenty-five years, their governments have tended to regard the preservation of good Anglo-American relations as more important than the merits of almost any individual cause of dispute.[1]

Similar considerations apply to a number of Commonwealth and European countries and anyone with practical experience of the extent to which friendly relations can facilitate intercourse between governments will under-

[1] There are naturally exceptions, of which the Suez Crisis of 1956 was one.

stand how easily the maintenance of such relations can become an objective in its own right. It is, nevertheless, an objective which has to be weighed against the other components of policy, lest ends should be sacrificed to means. Goodwill of this kind, though often powerfully reinforced by popular sentiment based on similarity of language, custom, ancestry or civilization, rests most securely on common interests and is necessarily vulnerable either to changes in the basic interests of the States concerned or to any reluctance by either side to maintain its contribution to the balance of mutual concessions. It is accordingly insufficient for the British Government, when contemplating the possibility of dispute with some friendly country, to assess British diplomatic capacities only in relation to the specific question at issue. 'On its merits', there may have been an administrative case for defending the conduct of British immigration officials towards Miss Eriksson[1]: in terms of the resulting loss of Swedish goodwill this seems rather more questionable.

Although, therefore, the national capacity for the advantageous resolution of disputes is highest in the case of friendly governments, this is subject to two limiting factors. Firstly, whenever this capacity is employed to obtain a concession (including such favours as diplomatic support in British disputes with third parties) from the foreign government concerned, this concession constitutes a draft on the fund of goodwill. If this fund is not periodically replenished by British concessions, a depletion of goodwill must follow and there will be a corresponding decline in the British national capacity in this field. Friendly relations may make it much easier to extort, by purely diplomatic pressure, a concession from a reluctant foreign government, but the ultimate cost of this immediate advantage may be greater.

The second limiting factor is British public opinion. In disputes conducted by diplomatic methods much can be,

[1] See Chapter 1.

and normally is, achieved by rational argument, by quiet persuasion, by appeals to interest or to sentiment. The great majority of disputes among friendly nations are resolved without public opinion ever becoming aware of their existence. When this kind of diplomacy fails, however, it may become necessary to contemplate other means of pressure: to threaten publicity, to conjure up the spectre of popular indignation in Britain, to hint at economic or administrative reprisals, even to suggest the possibility of a resort to military coercion. All such threats, whether implied or open, depend for their credibility and effect upon the presumed readiness of British public opinion to acquiesce in their employment. To take an extreme case, it is difficult to imagine any dispute in which a British Government could credibly hint at the remotest possibility of employing armed force against New Zealand. Similarly, in the more ordinary case of the dispute over British import surcharges with the governments of the European Free Trade Association, the effectiveness of British diplomatic efforts was diminished because the protests of these governments received widespread public support in Britain itself.

These examples illustrate the importance, in a negative sense, of the moral category of national capacities. The word 'moral', in this context, has no necessary connexion with 'right' or 'wrong', but is used to describe the sense of national purpose and determination which Napoleon had in mind when he said that, in war, moral considerations accounted for three-quarters and the balance of forces only for the other quarter. If the policy of a British government does not appear to reflect a sense of national purpose and determination, then British diplomatic representations will lack the reinforcement they might otherwise have derived from the moral capacities of the nation. Foreign governments will conclude that the British Government are unlikely to resort to economic or military sanctions, because such extreme measures would not receive the support, perhaps not even the acquiescence, of the British people. Foreign governments may also take the view that their resistance to British diplomatic representations will not, in the long run, even deprive their country of British friendship, esteem and consequent goodwill.

With a minority of friendly countries, therefore, the British Government can rely on extensive national capacities of a diplomatic character but must be careful, in so doing, neither to make disproportionate demands on foreign goodwill, nor to press a dispute further than is acceptable to British public opinion. In such cases, moreover, the capacity arising from the existence of friendly relations may itself exercise a positive influence on the formation of policy.

If, in 1968, Albania must be regarded as entirely inaccessible to British diplomatic influence, whereas Denmark may be considered as favourably disposed towards any British representations not actually injurious to Danish interests, the reactions of the great majority of foreign governments are less easily predictable. Though some may approach these two extremes in their general attitude towards Britain, there are many in which the degree of cordiality or hostility fluctuates very considerably and others where an indifferent neutrality is fairly constant. In such cases there is no reliable fund of goodwill on which to draw and the British diplomat must appeal to interest, to fear or to sentiments unconnected with friendship for Britain. If such governments cannot be persuaded that the concession desired by Britain would actually be in their own interest, or correspond to sentiments of their own, then counter-concessions must be offered or counter-measures threatened.

Such threats need not be overt, in which case their employment would constitute a call on a different category of the national capacities. Sometimes even an unfriendly government can be influenced by the mere threat of British displeasure. In 1884, for instance, the British Chargé d'Affaires at Athens was assaulted, while taking an afternoon stroll, by a Greek policeman. Without employing threats, or even consulting the Foreign Office in London, the Chargé d'Affaires was able to obtain from a reluctant Greek Government an apology and the public dismissal, in the presence of the British Consul and of a band playing God Save the Queen, of the offending policeman.[1] One may suppose that Greek compliance with demands which even the Foreign Office thought 'went a little beyond what was quite necessary' was prompted by recollection of Lord Palmerston's reaction, thirty-five years earlier, to the maltreatment of a Portuguese Jew whose birth in Gibraltar had given him British nationality. Before 1914 there were many foreign countries whose governments, though not necessarily animated by any sentiment of friendship or esteem for Britain or the British people, regularly proved responsive to British diplomatic representations. As a result, the mere presence of a British Ambassador or Consul in a particular country constituted an important asset and increased the national capacity in foreign affairs. Nowadays, of course, the intrinsic value of diplomatic representation has greatly declined. British dipomats abroad no longer inspire awe, but are regarded as scapegoats or, in the more suggestive French phrase, Boucs Emissaires,[2] for foreign displeasure and there are relatively few countries outside Western Europe which have not indulged in the safe and stimulating diversion of assaulting or insulting these unfortunate officials in the course of the last two decades.

The increasing inability of British diplomacy to protect either its own representatives or other British subjects overseas against the consequences of foreign displeasure is only partly due to a decline of British economic and military capacities relative to those of other States. If a

[1] See Harold Nicolson, *Lord Carnock*, Chapter III (Constable 1937).

[2] Literally 'envoy goats'.

United States warship were again forcibly to remove two American citizens from a British ship on the high seas, the British Government could obviously no longer, as they did in 1861, contemplate going to war to secure their return, a result then achieved by mere diplomacy, re-inforced by the dispatch of the Guards to Canada. But, if the thought of British displeasure no longer deters even weak and unprotected States from molesting British subjects, this is primarily due to a decline in British moral capacities. Once again, this is not a matter of 'right' and 'wrong'. There are plausible arguments of an ethical character against bombing the palace of a President to punish him for permitting the destruction of a British Embassy; there are practical arguments against the institution of an embargo on trade or even the withdrawal of aid. The British public are easily persuaded, in such cases, that acquiescence would be less inconvenient than active resentment. Foreign governments, however, tend to interpret such decisions as reflecting the absence of any national determination to protect British representatives, British subjects or British interests abroad. It is in this sense that there has been a decline in the moral capacities of the British nation and, consequently, in British diplomatic capacities as well.

This decline, curiously enough, has been accompanied by an increase in the importance attached to the maintenance of diplomatic relations for their own sake and irrespective of any benefit these can be supposed to afford. Friendly relations, it was earlier argued, are of intrinsic value, because they so greatly facilitate the avoidance and resolution of disputes. In Peking, however, the presence of a British Chargé d'Affaires has, in recent years, seemed more calculated to provoke than to resolve dispute. Nevertheless, recent British governments, in contrast to the attitudes adopted in earlier years,[1] have appeared to attach

[1] The British Minister was withdrawn from Washington on several occasions during the nineteenth century.

overriding importance to the maintenance of diplomatic relations in all circumstances and with all countries. In 1968 a Labour Foreign Secretary took a slightly defensive attitude on this question. He said:

> 'I have welcomed, not always with the full support of the entire House, the resumption of diplomatic relations with the United Arab Republic and the return of the Lebanese and British Ambassadors to London and Beirut.
>
> 'I am glad to be able to tell the House – again all the House may not like to hear this – that there are signs that others of the Arab countries which broke off diplomatic relations with us would be glad to resume them.'[1]

As a previous Conservative Government had insisted on maintaining diplomatic relations with Indonesia after the systematically organized destruction, in 1963, of the British Embassy and much other British property in Djakarta, it was presumably not from the official Opposition that Mr. Brown expected objections, nor were any in fact expressed by subsequent speakers in this debate. In view of this relative unanimity, therefore, it may suffice simply to note that the maintenance of diplomatic relations has recently become an objective in its own right and is thus capable of influencing policy.

Otherwise the most important feature of the diplomatic category of British national capacities is that, with the exception of a handful of friendly countries, the availability of diplomatic resources in any particular dispute almost always requires individual and *ad hoc* assessment. There is no longer any general disposition to regard concessions to Britain as reliably productive of material reward, nor to consider rebuffs to Britain as inherently dangerous. Most foreign governments, therefore, treat each British diplomatic representation on its merits and, if no other considerations influence them to make a concession, will do

[1] *Hansard*, 24 January 1968.

so only in return for immediate reward or in response to a specific threat.

This has had an apparently paradoxical consequence. In former times, when British governments readily resorted to economic or military sanctions, far more could be obtained by purely diplomatic means than is the case today. This is often not understood by critics of the 'weakness' of British diplomacy, who simultaneously expect British Ambassadors to 'take a strong line' with some erring foreign government, yet oppose any approach to the only policy that could make such a strong line effective – consistent, resolute and, if necessary, forcible support for British diplomatic representatives overseas. A polite request from the representative of a government known to back its words with deeds carries more weight than any amount of sound and fury in the absence of such a reputation.

Deeds, of course, can be of two kinds: economic and military, though the former is often the foundation of the latter, as appeared when British military intervention in Egypt in 1956 was inconclusively abandoned in the face of a run on the pound. But both expedients are subject to the same fundamental rule: power, in international disputes, is neither intrinsic nor absolute, but consists in the ability to apply appropriate force about a given point.

In 1951, for instance, when the seizure of the Abadan refinery provoked a dispute between the governments of Britain and Iran, which was ultimately determined by the application of economic sanctions, it was irrelevant that the economic resources of Britain greatly exceeded those of Iran. What mattered was that Britain was able to do without Iranian oil and, by enlisting the support of the major international oil companies, to deny to Iran any significant revenues from the oil she had seized. Even so, this was not a form of pressure which Britain could apply unaided and, when the moment came for a settlement, the

British owned Anglo-Iranian Oil Company had to surrender a large proportion of its interests to those foreign oil companies which had provided such indispensable assistance.

In this case, however, Britain was able to apply appropriate force about the point at issue. When successive Burmese governments sequestrated, generally without any pretence at adequate compensation, the property of British firms and British subjects in Burma, no similar expedients were available to the British governments concerned. Burma, though far poorer relative to Britain than Iran, was not dependent on the export of any particular product exposed to British sanctions. A trade embargo would have hurt Britain more than Burma and British aid to Burma was of insufficient importance for its withdrawal to constitute an effective bargaining counter. As a result the grievances of British subjects with interests in Burma remained unredressed and the subject of dispute.

It does not follow, however, that economic pressure, even when this can effectively be applied at a vulnerable point, will invariably produce the desired result. Rhodesia, for instance, has been subjected to economic pressure more extensive and prolonged than any previously attempted in peacetime. Yet, although these measures followed two years of equally vigorous and sustained diplomatic pressure, they have not yet produced the desired concessions from the Rhodesian Government. In spite of the similar failure of sanctions against Italy in 1935, this outcome seems to have been unexpected by the British Government. In January 1966, for instance, the British Prime Minister predicted that:

> 'The cumulative effects of the economic and financial sanctions might well bring the rebellion to an end within a matter of weeks rather than months.'[1]

[1] Communiqué of the Lagos Conference of Commonwealth Prime Ministers, 12 January 1966.

This is such an interesting example of overestimating the effectiveness of diplomatic and economic pressure that it deserves a brief digression into the subject matter of later chapters in order to illustrate how the theoretical concepts so far examined might have been employed in order to facilitate a more accurate assessment.

Bearing in mind that the effectiveness of pressure is measured at the point of application and has no necessary relationship to the weight, whether absolute or relative, of the capacities sustaining it, the starting-point for such an assessment must naturally be in Rhodesia rather than in Britain. It was from the Rhodesian Government that concessions were required and it was to them that pressure was to be applied. The first step must accordingly be to examine, from the Rhodesian standpoint, the nature and extent of the concessions sought. As the composition of that government, and of the ruling class that sustained it, was predominantly British, the theoretical factors relevant to British policy can be assumed, with greater safety than would be true of many foreign countries, also to apply to Rhodesian policy. The Rhodesian Government presumably regard Rhodesian national interests as requiring the maintenance, to the extent compatible with preservation of the existing social order, of the independence and authority of the nation-state. There is an obvious conflict between these objectives and the concessions demanded by the British Government, as embodied in the famous Six Principles. In essence these demanded:

> Unimpeded progress to majority rule; guarantees against amendment of the constitution; immediate improvement in the political status of the African population; ending racial discrimination; independence only on a basis acceptable to the people of Rhodesia as a whole; regardless of race, no oppression.

These six principles were originally put forward by the British Government as conditions for their formal recognition of Rhodesian independence. When this was unilaterally proclaimed by the Rhodesian Government, a further demand was made for the temporary surrender of independence and authority pending the introduction of measures to modify the existing social order in the sense required by the six principles.[1]

Whatever their abstract merits, these were considerable concessions to ask of the Government of what was, in fact if not in legal theory, an independent state. No comparable concessions had been demanded of any government in Britain since 1688. Then, although the concessions sought were supported by the majority of the ruling class and were directed to the restoration, rather than the transformation, of the existing social order, it required armed foreign intervention, civil war and the overthrow of the Government to reimpose Protestant Majority Rule and to deny civil rights to religious minorities. In 1899, when the British Government wished to modify the existing social order in the Transvaal and the Orange Free State by securing civil rights for British minorities, success was only achieved by a long and costly war, the annexation of both States and a prolonged period of military occupation. Later in the century efforts to impose Catholic Majority Rule throughout Ireland or to deny unrestricted independence and authority to the southern part of the island had to be abandoned after years of bitterness and strife of which the scars remain to this day.

When stated in theoretical terms and compared with a few of the many historical precedents available, it thus becomes obvious that the concessions demanded of the Rhodesian Government entailed a partial surrender of the power and privileges, not only of the Government, but also of the ruling class from which they derived their authority and which, in their eyes, constituted the nation-state. This surrender, moreover – and here we pass from

[1] Rhodesia: Proposals for a Settlement 1966: Command 3159 of December 1966. H.M.S.O.

national interests to national aspirations – was to be in favour of people who, though inhabiting the same country, were regarded by the ruling class as alien and incapable of assimilation to their ranks. Moreover, as these aliens greatly outnumbered the ruling class, this initial surrender would inevitably lead – indeed, was expressly intended to lead – to the ultimate emergence of a situation in which the composition of the ruling class reflected that of the population as a whole.

Concessions of this magnitude are sometimes made by a ruling class as the only apparent alternative to a complete loss of power and privilege, but the effectiveness of this incentive depends on the conviction, firstly, that an acceptable degree of power and privilege will remain and, more importantly, that the threat to total power and privilege is both real and imminent. Arguments based on long-term predictions seldom carry the same conviction because, as the late Lord Keynes was fond of remarking, in the long run we shall all be dead. The Rhodesian Government were thus little influenced by the argument that immediate concessions would avert the ultimate loss of all power and influence by the ruling class. Instead they deduced, from observation of developments in other African countries, that partial surrender rapidly led to total loss, and, from the situation in their own country, that there was no immediate threat to the existing social order. Even if a reasoned analysis of the national interest had been the only factor determining Rhodesian policy, it would have been difficult to refute these short-term arguments. But, when reason was reinforced by national aspirations of the kind already noted to be the most potent – negative and emotional – it must have been obvious to the British Government that severe pressure would be required to extort the concessions desired.

This pressure was initially diplomatic and, in so far as its character can be deduced from public statements, took three forms: argument, appeals to allegiance and threats.

The failure of all three was predictable: of argument, because it had to be based on long-term predictions; of allegiance, because this depends on protection, which successive British governments had denied; of threats, because the Rhodesian Government did not believe these to command the determined support of the British people. Indeed, the promptness with which economic pressure was applied after the Rhodesian declaration of independence suggests that the British Government had foreseen that diplomacy would be unavailing, even though its resources had been deployed with considerable vigour and virtuosity. When, therefore, Mr. Wilson predicted the end of the rebellion 'within a matter of weeks rather than months', he presumably expected the rapid development of a situation in which the Rhodesian ruling class would see no alternative to concessions hitherto regarded by them as inconsistent with their national interests and aspirations. In what circumstances could such a situation reasonably have been expected to arise and how could this have been produced by economic sanctions?

The two most obvious contingencies are excluded by the time factor. There was no likelihood that Rhodesian stocks of ammunition, spare parts and petroleum products would be so rapidly depleted as to produce, even within months, a situation in which the ruling class would no longer be able to maintain their authority over the rest of the population. Even insurgent groups have seldom experienced much difficulty in obtaining the necessary minimum of such supplies and this was a government known to command the sympathy of governments in limitrophe countries. Nor, in this predominantly agricultural country, could there be any real probability of starvation on a scale capable of threatening the ascendancy of the ruling class.

The only remaining contingency, and that presumably expected by the British Government, was the development of a situation in which the Rhodesian Government would prefer – or would be compelled by their own ruling class – to make political concessions in order to curtail economic losses. Before considering how the British Government might have expected such a state of affairs to be created by sanctions, it is worth restating the theoretical principle involved: the primary concern of any government is normally to preserve their own authority unimpaired and even a partial surrender of authority is seldom made except as the only means of avoiding a total surrender. In this case, however, there was no prospect of the mass of the people being able to threaten the Government with a total loss of power. Only the ruling class could do that. If, therefore, the ruling class wanted the Government to make concessions, there was a reasonable prospect of the Government maintaining their authority, even in diminished form. Indeed, if the desire of the ruling class for concessions was very marked, then concessions might offer the Government the only hope of retaining any authority at all. On the other hand, if any substantial section of the ruling class was opposed to concessions, then these would not only entail a surrender of authority over the mass of the people (the object, so far as the British Government were concerned) but also over the ruling class. Indeed, if the opposition were strong enough, the result could only be the loss of all authority by the Government. If there was any prospect of this, the main incentive for concessions – the retention of as much authority as possible – would disappear.

The theoretical question relating to the efficacy of economic sanctions was thus: would these create conditions in which the Rhodesian Government would expect to retain more authority by making concessions than by refusing them? Or, to put the same question in different terms, in what circumstances would a government making concessions command more effective support from the ruling class than a government refusing concessions?

The answer, obviously, must be that a ruling class will normally support the Government and the policy most likely to preserve their own ruling position. In some countries this ruling position depends primarily on the possession of wealth: rich people belong to the ruling class, but the poor do not. In such countries the impoverishment of the ruling class impairs the basis of its rule and narrows the gap dividing rulers and ruled. This may, however, be a lesser evil than certain kinds of economic crisis. It is better to lose some money – by submitting to higher taxes, for instance – than to risk a situation in which all money will lose its value because of revolution or catastrophic inflation. On the other hand, if wealth is the basis of power, it may be worth sacrificing some power in order to preserve wealth, because the retention of wealth offers a prospect that the surrender of power will indeed only be partial and perhaps even temporary. Ruling classes deriving their power from wealth are thus sensitive to considerations of economic advantage and readily adapt their political attitudes accordingly.

In many countries, however, the power-basis of the ruling class is different: the army, the Communist Party, a religious organization. Such countries will cheerfully ruin their balance of payments, put up with inflation, ban the sale of luxuries or introduce rationing: to buy armaments, preserve the unity of the party or uphold religious doctrine. They are relatively insensitive to considerations of economic advantage, because these do not determine the membership or privileged position of the ruling class. As long as being a colonel means being a member of the ruling class, it scarcely matters whether the colonel is personally poor and rules over a poor country: he will still enjoy the same relative power and privilege.

Within every ruling class, of course, there are divisions. Some members develop motives and interests independent of their power-basis: a particular colonel may become keener on acquiring imported luxuries than on maintaining the unity and ascendancy of the officer corps. If these tendencies are widespread, a situation may develop in which the divisions within the ruling class are more important than the division between that class and the rest of the people. If external pressure is applied to such a class, at least some elements are likely to favour concessions, either because these correspond to their own extraneous interests, or else because concessions seem necessary to preserve an already precarious class-unity. This is most likely to happen when the dissident element within the ruling class is either large enough to form a new class of its own or is counting on allies outside the ruling class.

The membership and privileged position of the Rhodesian ruling class were determined not by wealth, but by race. A white man belonged to the ruling class, a black man did not. The mere impoverishment of the ruling class would not affect this state of affairs. Some members of the ruling class, particularly those directly dependent on external transactions for their personal wealth, might nevertheless lose power and privilege, not in relation to the African majority, but in relation to other members of their own class. If there were enough of these people to form a new ruling class or if they could expect to find adequate allies outside the white population of Rhodesia, then the impoverishment resulting from the imposition of sanctions might constitute a sufficient incentive for the disruption of the existing ruling class and the emergence of a new government prepared for concessions.

When the problem is stated in these terms, it becomes obvious that the questions to be asked were: is there a group in Rhodesia which would be prepared to sacrifice a degree of white supremacy to preserve prosperity; would this group be capable of creating a new ruling class; what degree of impoverishment would at once spur the group into action and enable them to enlist sufficient allies to command success?

It is unlikely that questions of so theoretical a character were ever put to the British High Commissioner in Salisbury. Instead it seems probable – though this we shall not know until the archives are opened at the end of the century – that the problem was examined primarily from the British standpoint: what did the British Government want and how far were they prepared to go? The High Commissioner would then have been told the nature of the sanctions proposed, together with the results indicated by statistical projection, and asked to assess their local economic and political consequences. This would have been a difficult task. When an external force acts upon a human society, the latter can react in different ways: it is not inert and predictable. Experience may enable the observer to guess the likely reactions to an immediate impact – a megaton bomb, for instance. But, when the external force acts gradually and cumulatively – as do economic sanctions – the accuracy of prediction necessarily decreases with every day that passes, because a gradual force gradually transforms the society upon which it operates. The practical man of affairs, who relies only on experience and knowledge, may thus fall into error by neglect of the Newtonian principle: to every action there is an equal and opposite reaction. Moreover, one practical man will consult other practical men with knowledge and experience: bankers, businessmen, prominent importers, leaders of the opposition. These are likely not only to fall into the same theoretical error – the assumption of a constant frame of reference – but are likely to compound it by personal bias. Men do not make money unless they value money and, the more they make, the more they fear to lose it. As Mr. Lloyd George, then Chancellor of the Exchequer, remarked of reactions in the City of London to the declaration of war in 1914: 'financiers in a panic do not make an heroic picture'. Unassisted by theory, therefore, the best available practical knowledge and experience might well have combined to predict the success, perhaps even 'in weeks rather than months', of the Pragmatic Sanctions. But the theorist might have remembered that Lloyd George's description of dismay and despair among the bankers was balanced by the comment that: 'there was no sign of panic on the part of the public in a situation that for us as a nation was unprecedented'.[1]

The Rhodesian situation, however, was not unprecedented. On the contrary, it was a classical case of a ruling class faced with a demand for concessions involving a loss of power as well as of privilege. It was a case aggravated by the existence, in the eyes of this ruling class, of an unbridgeable gap between themselves and the rest of the population. It was a case in which the factor unifying the ruling class and distinguishing it from the rest of the population was not a mere matter of relative wealth, education, custom or even religion. All these can shade imperceptibly into one another. In 1830 a foreigner unacquainted with Britain might have had difficulty in distinguishing between the Duke of Wellington and Mr. Brougham; in 1945 between Mr. Churchill and Mr. Attlee; in 1966 between Mr. Heath and Mr. Wilson. But even a Martian would have noticed the difference between Mr. Smith and his African rivals. In such circumstances and irrespective of the morality or merits of the issues involved, theory and precedent indicate that, where national interests and national aspirations demand the same objective, this is likely to be pursued to the moral, rather than the economic or military, limits of the national capacity. On the face of it – and it must be emphasized that any final conclusion must wait upon events no less than on the publication of the official archives – this seems to be a case in which insufficient weight was given to the theoretical concepts which history suggests as likely to determine the reactions of governments and of ruling classes, particularly those of predominantly British composition.

[1] David Lloyd George, *War Memoirs*, Chapter IV (Odhams Press 1938).

There may, however, have been another factor involved. Contemporary British governments do tend to overestimate the influence exercised upon foreign governments by the conventional arguments of economic advantage. This is because these arguments often possess greater importance in Britain itself than in most other countries. Britain is exceptionally dependent on international trade and on international financial transactions, not only for the maintenance of the general standard of living, but also for the preservation of the existing social order. The mass of the people rely on imports for the necessities of life, for the maintenance of their employment and for a wide range of luxuries now so much a part of the 'British way of life' as to seem almost necessities. Any restriction on the availability of imports thus has swift and widespread repercussions on the entire British people. The complete denial of all imports for any significant length of time might lead to starvation and anarchy and, if Germany had ever seemed likely to attain this objective during the Second World War, the British Government would probably have had to sue for peace. Even the reduction actually achieved by German efforts compelled the British Government, unlike most of the other belligerents, to introduce measures of rationing and control so drastic as to result in important changes in the social order. These changes, by increasing the size of the ruling class and the expectations of the mass of the people, have made post-war governments far more sensitive than their predecessors to even minor fluctuations in the standard of living, let alone to the prospect of mass unemployment or rationing that might result from a significant reduction in the availability of imports. This sensitivity is further increased by the importance, not only to the economy but, above all, to the existing social order, of international financial transactions. At the time of the Suez Crisis the loss of £100 million from the reserves during November 1956 was regarded as an important argument for accepting a cease-fire, although this sum represented only about ten days' imports. Subsequent British governments have proved equally ready to modify their domestic and foreign policies at foreign bidding when sterling has come under pressure on the exchanges.

It is important to realize, however, that this British sensitivity to financial pressure is a political and not an economic phenomenon. Even during the worst periods of the war, when import restrictions and the diversion of domestic resources to military effort were at their height, the British people were never within measurable distance of seeing their standard of living fall to the average enjoyed by the human race. Since the war there has never been a moment when the difficulties of the British economy could not have been resolved by what most foreign governments would consider minor restrictions on the import of luxuries. It is to preserve the social order – and their own authority over the people – and not from sheer economic necessity, that successive British governments have made concessions. What mattered was not the extent of foreign pressure, but the influence of British public opinion. As was demonstrated during the Second World War, the British people are capable of withstanding far greater economic pressures than any since successfully exerted, provided, but only provided, that they consider the objectives of their Government to deserve national sacrifice.

Any attempt, therefore, to assess the vulnerability of foreign governments to economic pressure must ignore contemporary British precedents and concentrate on an analysis of the particular circumstances of that Government, an analysis in which political factors will generally be more important than economic. The crucial question must always be: can the foreign government concerned maintain their authority over their own people in the face of whatever economic pressures can be applied? This depends on many factors: the degree to which the standard of living depends on imports, whether these imports are of necessities or of luxuries, whether they benefit the mass of the people or only the ruling class, whether the ruling class are united. Broadly speaking, however, the lower the popular standard of living and the smaller the ruling class, the less vulnerable will be the Government to purely economic pressures. A low standard of living implies a low level of political influence; a small ruling class can more easily preserve its own power and privileges. In India and China, for instance, hundreds of thousands may actually die because of statistically minor variations in domestic production or imports. Yet their governments are less sensitive to external economic pressures than that of Britain, where death by starvation has not been a predictable result of Government policy, except for isolated individuals, during the present century. As a general rule, economic pressure is only effective when it either threatens the ascendancy of the ruling class or else creates serious divisions within it.

In Iran, for instance, the denial of revenue from oil exports did not prove effective until dissensions within the ruling class had led to the fall of Dr. Mussadiq. In Indonesia economic privation was a major factor in the downfall of President Sukarno and the subsequent modification of his anti-Western policies. But this economic privation (which was the result of his own mismanagement rather than of any deliberate pressure by foreign governments) had no influence on his own policies as long as he remained in power. Indeed, it would be difficult to quote any instance since 1945 in which a foreign government have been compelled, simply by British economic pressure, to make any major modification of their policy. To achieve this, it is normally necessary to bring about the fall of the Government concerned, which presupposes that the original policy of that Government either failed to command the united support of the ruling class or, at least, was not regarded as indispensable to the preservation of their power and privileges.

Economic pressures may accordingly be regarded as effective only in those cases where the foreign ruling class concerned can more easily preserve their power and privileges by yielding than by resisting. The economic weapon is thus most useful for securing minor concessions from rich, democratic countries or as a means of overthrowing governments deriving an insecure authority from a divided ruling class.

It is also more effective when threatened than when actually applied. Let us suppose, for instance, that Lord Avon had decided to defy American economic pressure in 1956, had imposed exchange control and import restrictions, had threatened to repudiate British debts and had adopted an economic policy for Britain similar to that pursued during the middle thirties in Germany under the auspices of Dr. Schacht. Could the United States, even if they had so desired, have coerced Britain into submission by purely economic means? The actual application of economic pressures is often as damaging to those who inflict as to those who suffer them, a lesson learnt by the oil-producing Arab States in 1967. Similarly, Spanish claims to Gibraltar have not been advanced by their application of economic pressure, though the implicit threat of counter-measures (the loss of the British tourist trade) may well have deterred the Spanish Government pressing their claim to extremes. On the other hand, if the British Government were actually to prohibit British tourists from visiting Spain, there would be a manifest, rather than implicit, application of economic pressures. This would be a direct challenge to the authority of the Spanish Government, which might then feel impelled to resist, not because the claim to Gibraltar was necessarily considered more important than the tourist revenue, but simply to preserve their authority in the eyes of their own people.

The economic relationship between two countries is normally one of mutual advantage. As such it may help to promote friendly relations and to create a climate of opinion in which both governments seek to avoid disputes or, if these arise, to refrain from conducting them in a manner liable to jeopardize trade. But if, as often happens, the foreign government concerned attach less intrinsic importance to trade and to considerations of commercial advantage than do the British Government, then the existence of this trade will be a liability rather than an asset to Britain in the event of dispute. Indeed, just as the maintenance of friendly relations can become an objective of policy in its own right, so can the maintenance of trade. It follows, therefore, that the most important contribution which economic resources can provide for the furtherance of foreign policy is the ability to dispense with foreign trade. The more economically self-sufficient any country becomes, the greater the potential independence of its foreign policy.

Economic self-sufficiency can, of course, exist either at the high level enjoyed by the United States, whose wealth is increased by trade, but whose livelihood does not depend on it, or at the low level of some undeveloped country exporting primary products and importing either luxuries or capital goods. Both types of country can afford to sacrifice economic advantage to political objectives without jeopardizing the existing social order. This is why economic aid so seldom induces the recipient government to pursue policies welcome to the donor. By 1967, for instance, Britain had spent thousands of millions of pounds on aid to over seventy members of the United Nations, very few of whom had thereby been deterred from pursuing anti-British policies, some of them to the point of open violence. To most of these countries aid was welcome, either because it provided immediate luxury for the ruling class or because it offered the hope of greater future prosperity for the people. But it was not indispensable to the preservation of the existing social order and could thus be sacrificed – temporarily at least – whenever political exigencies so required. Even when the national interest was not directly involved, British economic assistance seldom seemed to exert much influence on the policy of foreign governments: in December 1967 less than a dozen recipients – and these members of the Commonwealth – supported the British Government on an issue of great importance to Britain, but little or none to them: the vote in the General Assembly of the United Nations on Gibraltar.

In most disputes, therefore, British economic capacities exercise a negative influence on British policy, because these capacities depend, to a greater extent than those of most countries, on the maintenance of international trade and of normal economic relations. Only when the British market provides a more or less irreplaceable outlet for a high proportion of a particular country's exports, or in other special circumstances, is this dependence reversed. And, even then, the crucial factor is political, rather than economic. If denial of the British market would jeopardize the existing social order in the foreign country concerned but not in Britain, then the British Government possess a bargaining counter. But the mere existence of a high level of trade has no necessary effect on political relationships. Before 1914 Britain exported more to Germany than to any other country except India and imported more than from any other country except the United States, but this trading partnership neither mitigated Anglo-German rivalry nor appeared to offer an alternative to war for the resolution of their disputes.

This political factor is equally important to the more familiar concept of total British economic capacity as a limiting factor on policy. The idea that economic capacities alone restrict the foreign, or even the defence, policy of the British Government is only valid in contingencies more extreme than those so far encountered in time of peace. A British Minister may say that the country cannot afford a particular policy, just as someone may say he has no time to read this book. Each means that there are other things he would rather do. Either may be right, but each is making a choice, not yielding to inescapable necessity. When it is possible to quantify the cost of a particular foreign policy – keeping British troops in the Persian Gulf, for instance, or imposing sanctions on Rhodesia – the true touchstone for comparison is not the gross national product or the budget or the balance of payments: it is the amount of national resources which it is politically tolerable for the British Government to divert from other purposes. Therefore, although decisions in foreign policy ought to be preceded by an assessment of their economic consequences, these depend for their significance on political rather than economic factors. For practical purposes the economic capacities of Britain constitute a limiting factor on foreign policy much less important than the domestic policies of the British Government.

This may appear a paradoxical proposition to advance in respect of a country dependent on imports for half its food and nearly all its raw materials and which exports over a fifth of the gross national product. There are obviously limits beyond which no British Government can afford to ignore purely economic considerations. The point is that these limits have never actually been approached in time of peace. There is scarcely any foreign policy remotely likely to be adopted by a British government of which the foreseeable cost could not be met by the sacrifice of a few luxuries – imports of tobacco, for instance – or by a further increase in agricultural production. It is often forgotten that a major war did not prevent Britain, between 1938 and 1958, from increasing from a third to a half the proportion of her food produced at home, while simultaneously achieving a 60 per cent growth in industrial output.

Economic capacities are, in practice, neither a major limiting factor on British foreign policy, nor do they offer more than occasional assistance in the furtherance of its objectives. To what extent do they provide motive forces capable of exerting a positive influence on policy? That British foreign policy since 1919 has been powerfully influenced by economic considerations is undeniable; that these have been related to economic capacities seems more debatable. Anyone endeavouring to add a pinch of thought to the sentimental pragmatism of foreign policy can only contemplate with awe, and sometimes with dismay, the total ascendancy of dogma in the economic field. There is apparently no inconsistency which British governments will not swallow, no burden they will not impose on the people, no sacrifice they will not make of interest or of aspiration, provided only that this conforms to the economic doctrine of the day. Free Trade, Protection, the Gold Standard, Exchange Control, Convertibility, the Sterling Area, the Balance of Payments, International Confidence in Sterling – the slogans flicker past with all the inconsequence of sub-titles on an unsynchronized film. Yet in their name millions of Britons have known hunger and despair, governments have fallen, promises been broken, treaties scrapped. To the layman the successive, the dismal, the contradictory dogmas of British bankers and official economists must sometimes appear as the profoundest and most potent expression of the national death-wish. Endlessly, yet each time in a different cause, they recapitulate the closing scene of Götterdämmerung. Watched by the gloating Hagen Britannia rides unflinching into the flames and the ravens flap home, sourly satisfied, one to the Bank of England and the other to the London School of Economics.

The most spectacular of all these performances was inaugurated in 1925, when the British Government decided to return to the Gold Standard at an inflated parity. As predicted by Lord Keynes, the unavailing Siegfried of this drama, the new rate could not be sustained without a reduction in wages leading inevitably to the General Strike of 1926. Exports were slashed, our defences starved, the dole-queues swollen, the social order itself brought to the extreme brink of peril so that, however briefly and spuriously, the pound might 'look the dollar in the face'.

Worse was to follow. As the British economy continued to wither beneath the blight of Gold, its cult was held to require not only the creation of unemployment in Britain, but also the reduction, at the behest of foreign bankers, of even the pittance doled out to these victims of dogma. On the 23rd of August 1931 the British Government received an ultimatum from the New York firm of J. P. Morgan and Company specifying the terms on which, provided these had the sincere approval and support of the Bank of England, loans might be granted to enable Britain to remain on the Gold Standard. This was too much for even a mesmerized government. Though still unable to resolve on action, most Ministers did at least decline responsibility for this surrender of national independence and authority or for the consequential sufferings of their countrymen. The Government fell, another was constituted to preserve the Gold Standard at any cost to the people and, within a month, precipitately abandoned it with results which, if they scarcely mitigated the miseries its maintenance had caused, were at least generally admitted to have been beneficial.

The sceptical reader will find a clear account of this unbelievable saga in Chapters XXVI, XXVII and XXIX of Sir Harold Nicolson's *King George V*.[1] It has since been repeated, diminuendo, on more occasions than it is endurable to recount. In each case the national interest has been sacrificed, not to theory, for the theoretical alternatives were clearly stated at the time, but to dogma. It follows, therefore, that the main economic influence on foreign policy must be ascribed, not to national capacities, but to national aspirations of an essentially mythological charac-

[1] Harold Nicolson, *King George V* (Constable 1952).

ter. It can only be hoped that these will eventually be countered – and the supposedly all-important deficit[1] in the balance of payments redressed – by an appeal to the hitherto untapped surplus constituted by the moral capacities of the British nation.

[1] In 1962 this deficit was precisely equivalent to an arithmetical device unfortunately inaccessible to the author in his harassed schooldays: 'the balancing item introduced to balance the account', see *Britain: An Official Handbook 1967*, published by the Central Office of Information.

5

NATIONAL CAPACITIES: MILITARY AND MORAL

'That nation which is more reckless, more determined, more willing to accept damage, or enjoys greater freedom in making threats, could have important superiorities in a parity situation, both in its foreign policy and in its capability for escalation dominance.'

Kahn[1]

THE subject of this chapter is British ability to employ armed force for the prevention, termination or limitation of disputes with other nation-states. This ability can be assessed in two ways. A British Foreign Secretary involved in, or foreseeing, a particular dispute may inquire whether the use of force would promote a solution. Or, bearing in mind that military capacities are created primarily to further foreign policy, he may want to know whether the general objectives of British policy are compatible with British military resources. These are different kinds of question, because the possibility of using force in a particular dispute is governed by the military capacity which already exists, whereas the balance between foreign and defence policy can, over a period of years, be adjusted in either direction: by contracting the objectives of foreign policy or by expanding military capacity. Both questions, however, can be approached by the same route: an examination of the various ways in which force can be employed in the avoidance, termination or limitation of disputes.

Broadly speaking, there are three such methods:

[1] Herman Kahn, *On Escalation*, Appendix (New York, Praeger 1965).

The Definitive Use of Force: the immediate use of local force to create or reverse a *fait accompli*.

The Purposeful Use of Force: the threat or application of limited force to change the policy or character of a foreign government.

The Desperate Use of Force: the threat or use of force on a scale, or for objectives, not restricted to the immediate cause of dispute.

Force is used *definitively*, when creating a *fait accompli* to which the foreign government concerned are either unable, or else unlikely, to react in a manner disproportionately damaging to British interests. In 1807, for instance, the mere existence of the Danish fleet was a cause of dispute, because it might have been employed, with or without the consent of the Danish Government, to assist Napoleon in waging war against Britain. This fleet was accordingly removed by the Royal Navy and, with it, the cause of dispute. But, nearly a century later, when Admiral Sir John Fisher recalled this precedent to King Edward VII and suggested a similar removal of the infant German fleet, the King growled: 'Fisher, you must be mad.'[1] The difference between these two cases – and it is a difference fundamental to the argument of this chapter – lay in the potential repercussions of such an act of force. In 1807 Britain had long been at war with France (though not, at that particular moment, with Denmark) and was already suffering all the inconveniences attendant upon this condition. Neither Danish friendship nor Danish hostility were particularly significant to Britain – except as these affected the use of the Danish fleet. Because Danish friendship would not have sufficed to keep the fleet out of Napoleon's hands, it was seized and the possibility of Denmark giving effect to her resentment was simultaneously removed. At the beginning of the twentieth century, however, Britain was not at war in Europe and

[1] Harold Nicolson, op. cit., Chapter XII.

the seizure of the German fleet would by no means have deprived Germany of effective outlets for her resentment. On the contrary, such a step might well have precipitated a major war, which did not then seem otherwise inevitable, a war in which Britain might have had few allies and Germany many. This precedent of 1807 was, however, followed in 1940, when Churchill ordered the seizure or destruction of accessible units of the French Navy.

Opportunities to settle a dispute by forcibly removing its cause are naturally more frequent in time of war, but Russian destruction of an American U.2 aircraft in 1960 and the seizure by the North Koreans of the U.S. monitoring vessel *Pueblo* in 1968 were examples of its peacetime application. In each case there was a dispute over the right of the United States Government to obtain information about military activities in a foreign State. In each case the dispute was forcibly terminated by the foreign government in a manner that left the United States Government with no other choice than acquiescence or war. It is this confrontation of an opponent with a *fait accompli* which he cannot undo and which he can only resent at wholly disproportionate cost, which constitutes the most effective and economical way of employing armed force for the resolution of international disputes. But the conditions for this definitive use of force are stringent. First of all, the objective must be one that can actually be secured by armed force without the co-operation of the foreign government concerned. Preventing a close approach to North Korean shores by the *Pueblo*, or similar vessels, was such an objective, but this kind of force would have been inappropriate if the objective had been American recognition of the North Korean Government or if the *Pueblo* had been capable of effective defence or liable to immediate rescue.

The second condition is that the foreign government should be unable, or unlikely, to retaliate in a manner more damaging than the original cause of dispute. There are many factors involved here: the relative capacities, both military and moral, of each government, the strength and dependability of their respective allies: the extent to which nationals or assets of one State are so situated as to be at the mercy of the other. Each case requires a separate assessment in order to predict the likely reactions of the Government against which force is employed. But there are certain generally applicable considerations: a resort to force is more likely to meet with acquiescence if it is immediate in its application, instantaneous in its effect and appropriate in its nature. Immediate application means before public opinion can be aroused, allies mobilized or the dispute inflated beyond its original proportions. Instantaneous effect means that, before resistance can be organized, the use of force settles the original cause of dispute in a manner which cannot be undone or reversed. The nature of the force employed must also be appropriate in the sense of being exclusively directed to the resolution of the particular dispute. Unless this is obvious to the victim government, the main motive for the latter's acquiescence – to avoid suffering further violence – will be impaired.

There are occasional exceptions to the rule of immediate application, when special circumstances make it unlikely that the victim government could actually profit from any respite either to organize an effective defence or to mobilize allies. The Indian seizure of Goa in 1961, for instance, was a successful application of definitive force to terminate a long-standing and much publicized dispute. But its success depended on its relatively instantaneous effect: if Portuguese troops had been able to sustain a prolonged defence from street to street and house to house, the risks of intervention by Portugal's reluctant allies would have been greater and the whole operation less attractive. Moreover the circumstances were most unusual, in that India's natural enemies were reluctant to assist Portugal and the latter's allies were unwilling to oppose India. British governments can seldom expect that a prolonged dispute will leave their opponent as friendless and as vulnerable as when the dispute began.

It follows, therefore, that the moment to consider the use of force is at the outset of a dispute. The longer the delay and the greater the resort meanwhile to diplomatic or economic pressures, the greater – and consequently the more dangerous – is likely to be the extent of the force ultimately required. Indeed, unless force is employed at an early stage, it can seldom be definitive and the strongest argument for its use thus no longer applies.

In practice, of course, it is exceptionally difficult for a British government to employ force in this expeditious and, therefore, economical and effective manner. Not only are British governments more subject than many others to the domestic inhibitions discussed in a later chapter, but their administrative and political structure makes it harder for them to reach a prompt decision or to take a timely initiative. Moreover, the widespread diffusion of British subjects and British assets abroad means that most foreign governments engaged in disputes with Britain possess an inherent advantage in the number of British hostages at their mercy. The definitive use of force is thus an expedient seldom available to twentieth-century British governments, but one which should always be considered, in the few cases where it is applicable, because of its exceptional economy and effectiveness.

Its main importance to foreign policy, however, is that it can easily be – and often is – employed against Britain. German reoccupation of the Rhineland in 1936, Albanian mining of the Corfu Straits in 1946 and the Chinese attack on H.M.S. *Amethyst* in 1949 are only some of the more dramatic instances of its employment to settle disputes against the wishes of the British Government. In each case the foreign government concerned could be sure that the first blow would confront Britain with a choice between acquiescence and escalation. Not every dispute lends itself to such expedients – even at the hands of foreign governments more favourably situated than most British governments – nor is the use of force by these governments invariably definitive, but there have been enough instances in recent times to reinforce the proposition advanced earlier: the time to consider the use of force is at the outset of any dispute. Even if a British initiative has to be excluded, it may be necessary to guard against the use of force by the other government concerned. It is imprudent to enter upon a dispute or to pursue policies liable to lead to dispute without first considering whether British military capacities are adequate to counter a possible resort to force by the other side.

In considering the defensive use of force, the same arguments apply: to be definitive this must be immediate in its application, instantaneous in its effect and appropriate in its nature. If a British ship is seized by a foreign government, for instance, the ideal counter-stroke would be its prompt rescue by the Royal Navy. If the United States had been able to recapture the *Pueblo* before she reached a North Korean port, the *fait accompli* would have been reversed, but, once the crew were beyond rescue, even retaliatory action was inhibited by the desire to save their lives: an objective which depended on the co-operation of the North Korean Government. Even if visible British precautions do not deter a foreign government from attempting the use of definitive force, this can still be frustrated if the defence is strong enough to prevent the rapid creation of a *fait accompli*. A British colony defending itself against foreign attack is in a very different position to one already overrun. The first case would leave a wide range of British options; the second might restrict these to a choice between acquiescence and war. In any dispute liable to invite the use of force by either side, the primary influence of military capacities does not depend on the total military potential of the two sides, but on their respective ability and readiness to apply immediate and appropriate force about the actual point at issue.

Unfortunately only an ideal government in an ideal world could hope so to order their policies as never to risk a dispute in which the immediate application of local force would not be advantageous. It is accordingly necessary to consider less direct applications of force, even though these are less likely to be efficacious. This secondary use of force can be regarded as *purposeful* to the extent that it is expected to prevent, determine or limit a dispute without thereby creating a new situation more unfavourable to Britain than the probable outcome of British concessions at the outset of the dispute. This was presumably the purpose of British armed intervention in the Suez dispute of 1956, but the result was unfortunate: Britain neither secured the concessions sought from Egypt (some of which might have been obtained by negotiation) nor avoided greater disadvantages than any likely to have followed an initial acquiescence. In the same year, however, Soviet armed intervention in Hungary determined a dispute in the sense desired by the Soviet Government without any important disadvantage to Soviet interests. The widely different results obtained in these two cases, as in the many other instances of the last two decades, suggest the need for some analysis of the theoretical requirements for the successful employment of purposeful force in settling disputes.

The starting-point must naturally be to define the objective, which is necessarily political rather than military because the kind of force now under consideration operates only indirectly. Force does not itself do anything: it induces somebody else to do something. This 'somebody else' may be a foreign government or it may be the leadership of an insurgent movement. In either case there is a group of people who take decisions and the purpose is to induce them to take a particular decision which they would otherwise have been unwilling to contemplate. In principle, of course, the most economical and effective method is to apply force to the decision makers themselves. They may be exposed to physical duress or they may be forcibly removed and replaced by others of a more amenable disposition. In 1942, for instance, a show of military force in support of the British Ambassador's representations to King Farouk was enough to bring about an advantageous change in the Egyptian Government. In 1944 the arrest of Admiral Horthy and some of his subordinates by German troops successfully prevented Hungary from seeking a separate peace. On the other hand, when Dutch forces captured President Sukarno and most of his government in 1948, this military success in no way advanced the political objectives of the Netherlands Government in Indonesia. Nor did the arrest and deportation, in 1956, of Archbishop Makarios prevent the continued erosion of British authority in Cyprus. The decisive factors in such cases appear to be the degree of support enjoyed by the foreign government from their own people and the unity of the foreign ruling class. In 1944, for instance, Admiral Horthy's apparent desire for a separate peace did not command public support because it had not been revealed to the Hungarian people, whose ruling class were divided between resentment of the Germans and fear of the Russians. There was thus little difficulty in assembling an alternative government more amenable to German wishes and commanding at least as much support. But, where the foreign government enjoy popular support for a publicly proclaimed policy and have the backing of a united ruling class, the members of this government are unlikely to be able – even if they were willing – to change their policy merely to avoid physical violence directed against themselves.

As a general rule governments as such are not vulnerable to foreign force unless their internal authority is already precarious. Even so, the use of overt force against an insecure government may actually create a nationalist reaction which has the effect of rallying support either for the Government or, if this is removed, for the policy of that government. It then becomes necessary, as happened in Hungary in 1956, to make much more extensive use of force to install a new government and to support their authority. Even with the very large forces then employed by the Soviet Government, this might not have been possible without substantial support from the Hungarian ruling class – the Communist Party.

It follows, therefore, that, before contemplating the use of force specifically against a foreign government, there must be a reasonable assurance that this could actually be replaced by another government able and willing to effect the desired change of policy. This assurance can most easily be provided if there exists in the foreign country concerned an organized group willing to take the initiative in coercing or replacing the Government. The use of force can then be confined to supplying arms, money or other forms of assistance not involving a direct and open affront to nationalist sentiment. Such methods offer the further advantage of making it less likely that other governments will come to the assistance of a victim government apparently unable to command the support of their own people. The covert promotion and support of an essentially indigenous *coup d'état*, revolution or counter-revolution is nearly always a better proposition than the overt intervention of alien forces. Since 1945 changes in the Governments of Czechoslovakia, Guatemala, Iran, Laos and Vietnam, to name only the most conspicuous cases, have been attributed to the covert intervention of foreign powers and, though some of these cases still await the judgement of historians, there is little reason to doubt that foreign influence can be decisive when the internal circumstances are favourable. Indeed, if it is impossible to proceed in this way, then it must generally be doubtful whether anything can be achieved by external force limited to the Government themselves.

In such cases an even more indirect use of force may be

contemplated. If there is no prospect of coercing the actual members of the foreign government, nor of replacing them by another government able and willing to take the desired decisions, it may nevertheless be possible to convince the offending government either that their present policy will be ineffective or else that it will expose their country to disproportionate damage. In 1948, for instance, the Soviet Government and their East German allies endeavoured to obtain concessions by imposing a blockade on West Berlin. This was successfully countered by the Western air-lift, which eventually convinced the Soviet Government that their blockade would be ineffective. It should be noted, however, that this expensive operation had to be maintained for nearly a year before even such a cautious government as that of the Soviet Union yielded to the logic of events. In the case of Indonesian 'confrontation' of Malaysia, President Sukarno continued his pin-prick attacks against Malaysian territory for nearly three years and gave no sign that the successful defence maintained by British and Malaysian forces had in any way diminished his determination to pursue this policy, which petered out only after he himself had fallen from power. The defensive use of force to convince a foreign government that their objectionable policy should be abandoned as ineffective is thus liable to be a slow and expensive process, particularly if the policy in question was originally adopted, as often happens, from essentially irrational motives. This expedient, moreover, is only available in those cases where the decision sought from the other government is negative: to stop doing something or to refrain from doing something. Even so, it can seldom be employed if the objectionable action takes place within the territory of the foreign State. It would not, for instance, have been possible to 'defend' the Suez Canal against President Nasser in 1956.

Nevertheless, when circumstances permit the defensive use of force, this has certain inherent advantages. In many cases it helps to limit the dispute. For instance, there are various British colonial territories claimed by other countries. If each of these territories is capable of resisting any likely surprise attack, then the foreign government concerned may be deterred from making the attempt. To ensure such a local defence may be an expensive process, but it will nearly always be cheaper than recapturing the territory once it has been overrun or than mounting retaliatory attacks elsewhere to persuade the foreign government to withdraw. Even if the presence of local forces fails to deter an attack, it may be possible to contain this and to remain on the defensive. This is often an unpopular policy with military commanders, who may see greater attractions in a counter-offensive. But the political advantages of a defensive policy are substantial. First of all it tends to limit the dispute and to discourage escalation. Secondly it ensures that the really difficult question – what to do next? – remains to be answered by the other side. During the Indonesian confrontation of Malaysia from 1963 to 1965 for instance, it soon became obvious that Indonesian attacks were failing to inflict any significant damage and that Indonesian casualties were far higher than those of the defenders. Nevertheless a purely defensive policy was tying up large numbers of British troops in Malaysia and costing the British taxpayer large sums of money. There must have been a considerable temptation for the British Government to order their forces to take the offensive. It would presumably have been easy to do great damage to Indonesian forces and even, if this had been desired, to the Indonesian economy and the Indonesian people. But would this have induced the Indonesian Government to change their policy or the Indonesian ruling class to change their Government? Dutch experience in Indonesia between 1946 and 1949 scarcely suggests this. Nor did the shattering defeat inflicted on Egypt, Jordan and Syria by Israeli forces in 1967 produce any lessening of Arab terrorist attacks against Israel.

And American bombing of North Vietnam only resulted in larger and more effective intervention by North Vietnamese forces in the South.

Naturally these three cases were very different and it would be wrong to suggest that the arguments for a defensive policy in Malaysia applied with equal cogency to Israel and to Vietnam. But defence succeeded, both militarily and politically, in Malaysia and, if this policy cost both time and money, the total casualties suffered on both sides during these three years of fighting were much less than those of a single week of the war in Vietnam.

Disputes can arise, however, in which the definitive use of force is not possible, in which there is no chance of coercing or replacing the foreign government and in which a purely defensive use of force, is either inapplicable (because definitive force has already been used by the other side) or unacceptable (perhaps because a prolonged defensive would entail a loss of authority by the British Government). In such cases it is necessary to consider the infliction of damage, not on the foreign government, but on their nation-state. In principle there should be a degree of damage which the Government concerned, or their ruling class, would consider less acceptable than making the desired concession. If this damage can be threatened or inflicted without fear of adverse repercussions and the victim government then makes the necessary concession, this is a purposeful use of force to resolve a dispute.

Such expedients were widely and often successfully employed during the nineteenth century. British maritime supremacy was exploited to extort concessions by the threat or use of naval blockade, naval bombardment or the seizure by naval landing parties of key towns, fortresses or installations. These methods had the military advantage that both the British Isles and British warships at sea were immune from retaliation, that the victims were incapable of ending or limiting the damage inflicted except by concession and that the British casualties and expenditure involved were usually unimportant. Even so, part of their success was due to political factors: the States against which such methods were employed seldom had governments commanding widespread popular support or even an efficient central administration. There was thus little risk that the infliction of damage, even if militarily irresistible, would evoke a popular resistance movement capable of nullifying any useful influence exerted on the actual rulers of the country. Similar considerations often promoted the success of a militarily more dubious expedient: the punitive expedition, which would often penetrate deep into the interior of a foreign country to destroy property and take prisoners. The most spectacular example, brilliantly described in Peter Fleming's *The Siege at Peking*,[1] was the international expedition of 1900, which relieved the beleaguered diplomatic missions in the Chinese capital and secured important concessions from the Chinese Government. Such expeditions, however, cost more in men and money than naval pressures, aroused greater foreign opposition and were sometimes repulsed. Moreover, the infliction of damage, whether by naval or by military means, was generally more successful in extracting immediate concessions than in effecting any lasting change in the policies of the foreign government concerned. It was often necessary to repeat the infliction of damage and sometimes to abandon this expedient in favour of the military occupation or annexation of the offending territory.

On the whole, however, the infliction of damage constituted, throughout the nineteenth century, a reasonably effective and economical method of extorting concessions from weak States, provided these were accessible by sea or from adjoining British territory. In 1896, for instance, thirty-eight minutes of naval bombardment sufficed to change the Government of Zanzibar. Since 1945, on the other hand, this method has seldom been successfully

[1] Peter Fleming, *The Siege at Peking* (Rupert Hart-Davis 1959).

employed, whether by British governments or by those of other countries enjoying greater military capacities or fewer inhibitions. The Chinese bombardment of Quemoy and Matsu in 1958 was far more violent and prolonged, but no more successful in extorting the desired concession, than the French bombardment of Sakiet (Tunisia) during the same year or the British bombardment of a fort at Harib (Yemen) in 1964. The most conspicuous failure, however, has been American bombing of North Vietnam, in which damage was inflicted on a larger scale and for a longer period than ever before, yet without extorting any concession from the victim government. Indeed, though other kinds of force have been successfully employed to serve political ends since 1945 – definitive force, defensive force, indirect coercion of a foreign government (Macao 1967), covert instigation of a *coup d'état* and even open intervention to replace a foreign government (Hungary in 1956 and the Dominican Republic in 1965) – it is difficult to find a single instance in which the mere infliction of damage has sufficed to extort concessions or to overthrow a government. Israel, for instance, has repeatedly resorted to this expedient and, in 1967, did so on a very large scale and with remarkable military success. Yet, although Israel's military position was undoubtedly improved by her victory, this neither put an end to terrorist attacks from her neighbours, nor induced them to offer concessions, nor resulted in the overthrow of hostile governments.

There are several reasons for this post-war decline in the efficacy of damage-infliction. Militarily the key factors have been the disappearance of the invulnerable fleet and the ease with which modern weapons can be acquired even by weak and impoverished States. When the Royal Navy blockaded Greece in 1850 there were no mines, torpedoes, submarines, aircraft or missiles to inhibit their operations, which were immune from any interference except that of a superior fleet – which did not exist. The British Government were thus able to employ limited force in complete confidence that its limits would continue to be set by themselves alone. Nowadays not even the strongest naval power could maintain close blockade of a hostile coast with impunity and the United States Government have learned in the hard way that it is not in their power to limit the cost or the repercussions of inflicting damage even on a weak and impoverished country.

This fundamental alteration in the technical aspect of military capacities has been further complicated by political changes. Damage-infliction, particularly for the British Government, is subject to severe domestic inhibitions, partly because of the disappearance of the naval blockade, which produced a high incidence of economic loss to the victim with few casualties and at little cost to the British Government. A still more important change, however, is in the international situation. As late as 1914 the infliction of damage on one State by another was widely regarded as acceptable, provided the operation was clearly of a limited character and prompted by some kind of provocation from the victim. That Austria should react to the murder of the Archduke Franz Ferdinand by issuing an ultimatum to Serbia did not in itself strike even Serbia's supporters as unreasonable: what precipitated the First World War was Austria's refusal to respect the conventional limits either in the extent of her demands or in her rejection of the substantial concessions offered by Serbia. Where the victim was outside Europe and not under the protection either of a European Power or of the United States, the infliction of damage in response to provocation was not merely acceptable to international opinion, but was sometimes encouraged and even supported by other governments. However much the Great Powers might quarrel among themselves, they tended to agree that they were collectively entitled to a degree of respect from weaker and less advanced countries. If one of these transgressed the accepted norms of international conduct, the infliction of punishment by the aggrieved

Great Power would seldom be opposed by other Great Powers unless their interests were directly affected. Nowadays the opposite is true. Almost any nation-state, however obnoxious or insignificant, and whatever the provocation it may have offered, can count on a degree of international sympathy and support if threatened with retaliation. The prevailing doctrine seems to be that the use of overt force by one nation-state against the territory of another is inadmissible, but that any form of offensive conduct short of this must be accepted, however reluctantly, as an inherent attribute of national sovereignty.

This doctrine would be less important if it were not reinforced by ideological conflicts and by the polarization of so many nation-states between the rival influences of the Soviet Union and the United States. Both these Super-Powers have a common interest in preventing or limiting conflicts liable to lead to a dangerous confrontation between themselves, but neither wishes to see its influence reduced by permitting the infliction of decisive damage on a client-state, whether actual or potential. Most governments threatened with damage can thus expect a degree of support from either the Soviet Union or the United States and some are sufficiently dexterous to obtain it from both – as did President Nasser in 1956. The victim of damage can thus often hope that its repetition will be prevented or limited by the intervention of one of the Super-Powers, who may tacitly recognize the right of each to discipline its own satellites, but who are not disposed to extend this to neutrals. The existence of this hope greatly reduces the effectiveness of damage as an incentive to concessions, as appeared when the Soviet Union intervened in 1967, not to prevent the infliction of damage on Egypt, Jordan and Syria (the Israelis moved too fast for that), nor to retaliate (the Arab States were only quasi-clients and Israel had a similar relationship to the United States), but to mitigate its consequences and discourage its repetition.

Finally, and this is the most important factor of all, most governments are nowadays more dependent than ever before on nationalist sentiment for the preservation of their authority. During the nineteenth century there were many parts of the world where nationalism scarcely existed as a political force and where governments could more easily preserve their authority by making concessions in the face of damage threatened or inflicted by a foreign government than by any attempt at resistance. This is seldom true today. Again and again, in different parts of the world, the infliction of damage by a foreign government has actually increased the degree of support enjoyed by the victim government and, consequently, their ability to refuse concessions.

Only in the most exceptional circumstances, therefore, can the deliberate infliction of damage in order to extort concessions from a foreign government be regarded as a purposeful use of force likely to be rewarded by success. A government enjoying precarious internal authority and lacking either adequate military resources or the favour of a Super-Power might be considered a suitable victim, but, even against such a government, other methods of employing force would probably be more effective. There may, however, be cases in which the threat, whether explicit or merely potential, of inflicting damage can constitute a deterrent to unfriendly action by a foreign government. Threats, particularly if these are discreet, may often arouse only fear: blows normally excite anger and resentment. Before 1939 the prospect of German air-raids had greater deterrent effect upon the British Government than their reality in 1940 and subsequent years. Such threats, however, have to be credible: the foreign government concerned must believe that the British Government would actually be prepared to inflict the specified damage, a condition which can seldom be met without publicity and all the repercussions this entails.

These are the principal expedients open to British

governments contemplating the use of force to resolve a dispute with a foreign government. The influence of military capacities on an existing dispute should accordingly be assessed by inquiring whether one of these expedients is politically feasible (both as likely to command domestic support and to have the desired effect on the dispute) and secondly, whether the military resources exist to apply it. In making any such assessment it will naturally be essential to take account of the capacities and likely intentions of the allies, actual or potential, of both sides. Experience suggests that friends will be more helpful, and enemies less belligerent, if the force employed is definitive, defensive or rapidly effective, than if it appears likely to involve the sustained infliction of damage.

In the longer term it is to support such uses of force that military capacities should be created. If this is impossible, then there is a case for modifying foreign policy to lessen the risk of disputes incapable of successful resolution by whatever military capacities it is actually decided to create.

These are not unreasonable objectives of policy. Although statesmen and historians usually prefer to describe British governments as resorting to force only when foreigners have left no other option open to them, this has not, even for practical purposes, actually been the case since 1745. In that year Prince Charles Edward, with some slight assistance from France, presented the Government of King George II with a genuine choice between relinquishing their domestic authority and resorting to force. On every subsequent occasion the British Government of the day could have kept the peace, perhaps at considerable cost to their external authority, by making concessions that would have preserved intact national independence, the social order and their own domestic authority. Even in 1914 and 1939 it was the British Government that declared war on Germany, not in order to avoid making concessions, but because these had been refused by the German Government. In great issues as in small, British resort to force has been a deliberate choice and such acts of policy must take account of national capacities as well as of national interests and aspirations. Neither the importance of an interest nor the strength of an emotion is rationally adequate to justify a resort to force unless this expedient is demonstrably likely to achieve the desired objective.

There have, however, been many instances in British history of the unsuccessful use of force, often leading to eventual settlement of a dispute on terms less favourable than those available at the outset. Sometimes these have been the result of mere military incompetence – a problem beyond the scope of the present work – but often the cause has been failure to envisage in advance the precise manner in which force was to be employed to secure the desired political objective. Even if Britain and France had been able, in 1956, to inflict on Egypt a military defeat as swift and decisive as that achieved by Israel in 1967, it does not follow that this would necessarily have produced what was presumably the desired result: Egyptian acceptance of international control over the Suez Canal. As a permanent occupation of the Canal Zone had earlier been found impracticable and experience, both in Egypt and elsewhere, suggested that foreign rule of Egypt would be even more difficult to maintain, the only practical alternatives were that President Nasser would change his policy or that he would be replaced by another Egyptian Government able and willing to do so. No evidence has yet been produced to suggest that either outcome could reasonably have been expected.

There may nevertheless be seemingly rational arguments for the employment of force without regard to its likely effect on the actual cause of dispute or to the prospects of military success. This is *the desperate use of force*, whether intended as an act of escalation, as a display of national resolution, or as a simple catalyst in a situation so adverse that any change seems likely to bring ultimate advantage. As all these objectives are of a somewhat indefinite character, it is often difficult to define in concrete terms the kind of situation which would be regarded as constituting attainment of the objective and still harder to predict the manner in which force might be employed to create this situation. The use of force for such purposes thus has no foreseeable limits either in extent or in duration. Nor can its consequences be predicted with any accuracy. For all these reasons it is properly described as a desperate expedient.

On 31 March 1939, for instance, the British Prime Minister told the House of Commons that:

> 'In the event of any action which clearly threatened Polish independence and which the Polish Government accordingly considered it vital to resist with their national forces, His Majesty's Government would feel themselves bound at once to lend the Polish Government all support in their power.'[1]

This was a classic example of threatening the desperate use of force. Nobody can seriously have expected that any likely threat to Polish independence could actually be resisted with the help of British force nor, when this contingency arose, was any attempt made to provide the Polish Government with effective support. This unsolicited and, to Poland, worthless guarantee was an act of escalation. It was also intended to display British resolution and to alter a situation which had enabled Germany to attain one objective after another in the face of impotent British protests. The result was a six-year war which, at great cost in British lives, lastingly impaired British national interests and left Poland with less independence at the end than at the beginning.

Not every resort to desperate force has quite such disastrous results. It is arguable, for instance, that the

[1] Churchill, *The Gathering Storm*, op. cit., Chapter XIX.

continued independence of Finland is due to her undoubtedly desperate decision to fight the Soviet Union in 1939 and again in 1941, in that this display of resolution convinced the Soviet Government, as nothing else would have, that the annexation of Finland (as happened to Estonia, Latvia and Lithuania) or her conversion into a Satellite (as happened to Bulgaria, Czechoslovakia, Hungary, Poland and Roumania) would be more trouble than it was worth. It is also possible to regard the Israeli attack on Egypt, Jordan and Syria in 1967 as a successful use of desperate force rather than as an abortive attempt at the purposeful infliction of damage. In each case the assumption turns on the argument that, without such a resort to force, the situation would have developed in a manner even more disadvantageous to Finland or to Israel. This argument is necessarily somewhat hypothetical. The concessions which Finland had to make to the Soviet Union in 1945 were more disadvantageous than those she refused in 1939, but the case for this initial refusal depends on the doctrine that any nation-state making one concession under pressure will subsequently be faced with further demands. Therefore, although Finnish concessions in 1939 would not, of themselves, have fatally impaired her national interests, acquiescence then would have been interpreted as a lack of the moral capacity to resist further, and more genuinely damaging, demands. This is a persuasive argument – familiar to English readers from the notorious analogy of King Aethelred's payment of Danegeld – but one which requires to be approached with great caution in any specific case. Literally interpreted, it would make any concession impossible and entail a state of perpetual war. There is thus a conflict between the immediate advantages of conceding a demand which cannot effectively be resisted and the longer term risks of thereby impairing moral capacities for future resistance. This is a dilemma which it should be one of the prime objectives of policy to avoid and in which decisions are more likely to be taken on emotional impulse than on the basis of any arguments susceptible to useful discussion here.

A different argument for the rational use of desperate force stems from the theory of escalation. This is a concept which has resounded, ominous yet undefined, in various passages of this chapter. Dr. Herman Kahn, the leading exponent of this theory, defines 'escalation' as 'a competition in risk-taking, or at least resolve'.[1] His argument is that, in a dispute between two nation-states, one may succeed in extracting concessions from the other by threatening or inflicting a degree of damage which the other is prepared neither to counter nor to match. At first sight this may seem to differ little from the expedient of damage-infliction, which was earlier held to be of little practical utility. But damage-infliction was considered as an example of the use of limited force, whereas escalation is a graduated approach to the use of unlimited force, in which the effect of each successive threat or act of violence depends less on the actual damage involved than on the increased credibility this lends to the underlying threat of virtually total destruction.

This relatively new doctrine is primarily based on the capacity of nuclear weapons for the immediate and irresistible infliction of damage to an extent never previously attainable. Before 1945 any threat of unlimited force was subject to two factors of uncertainty. Firstly, the threatening State might only be bluffing. Secondly, even if it attempted to implement the threat, it might fail. The invading army might be repulsed or the bombers shot down. Even an initial victory could still be reversed by the mobilization of fresh forces or the intervention of new allies on the other side. The threat of unlimited force then meant the threat of war, but the destruction wrought by war was seldom regarded as intolerable except to the defeated and few governments were ever convinced that

[1] Herman Kahn, *On Escalation*, op. cit., Chapter I.

defeat was inevitable. Small, friendless States might yield to an ultimatum from a much stronger power, but, between States that considered themselves at all equally matched, threats of war usually led to actual war: they did not deter because the results of their implementation seemed uncertain. When Chamberlain extended his guarantee to Poland, he probably hoped to deter Hitler from attacking that country. He failed because Hitler believed neither in Britain's resolve to carry out her threat, nor in her ability to inflict intolerable damage if she did.

Today, however, it is argued that any nuclear power is capable of inflicting, within a matter of minutes and with complete certainty, damage exceeding that suffered by any combatant in the Second World War. The Soviet Union and the United States could go even further, being capable of the immediate and complete destruction either of each other or of lesser nation-states. A government threatened with unlimited force by either Super-Power need only consider whether the ultimatum is seriously intended: if it is, then only concession can avert destruction. On the other hand, any government employing nuclear weapons would risk retaliation, if not from the victim, then from another nuclear power. If the Soviet Union and the United States were both involved, whether as principals or as allies, on opposite sides of the dispute, both would risk complete destruction. A mere threat from either might thus lack credibility, because the potential victim would ask: are they really prepared to risk their own destruction simply to extract this concession? Even in the absence of such a direct confrontation, there are so many possible deterrents to the use of nuclear weapons that the resolve of the threatening government is likely to be open to doubt. It is the purpose of escalation to erode such doubts and, by a series of increasingly reckless acts, to demonstrate such unlimited resolve that concessions will be made without the actual use of unlimited force.

The full ramifications of this theory should be studied in the indispensable, if difficult, pages of Dr. Kahn. Its relevance to American foreign policy need not be discussed here, but it has two obvious weaknesses as an expedient for use by British governments. The first of these is military: British nuclear capacities are not large enough in relation to British vulnerability to nuclear bombardment to make British threats of nuclear war credible in any but the most exceptional circumstances. The British Isles are too small and crowded for the independence, the authority or the social order of the British nation-state to survive an attack by any nuclear power capable of producing a dozen thermo-nuclear explosions in or over British cities. Even if many million British subjects managed to survive a nuclear war, the nation-state would not. Militarily, therefore, a British nuclear ultimatum would scarcely be credible unless employed against a country which could neither itself use nuclear weapons to retaliate nor rely on any other nuclear power to do so. Moreover, even if a serious dispute were to arise with such a country, it is not obvious that a process of escalation would increase British ability to extort concessions by threats. Each act of escalation might reinforce belief in the resolve of the British Government, but would also increase opposition, both domestic and international, to any use of nuclear weapons. Even if neither the United States nor the Soviet Union were initially prepared to deter the British Government by counter-threats, the likelihood of such a reaction would increase as escalation continued. A British Government might conceivably get away with a surprise attack, or an ultimatum of a few hours' duration, against a non-nuclear power without nuclear friends. It would take a little time for the two Super-Powers to establish that neither was covertly backing Britain (Marshal Bulganin did not make his veiled nuclear threat to Britain in 1956 until he was sure that the U.S. Government were not secretly supporting the Suez adventure) and, if the victim had surrendered or been destroyed before agreement could be reached on the 'hot-line', it is just possible that mere retaliation would then seem pointless. But the delay imposed by escalation would, at the very least, allow the intended victim to hope that one or even both of the Super-Powers would intervene in time to deter Britain from the actual employment of her nuclear capacities. Either could survive, as a nation-state, a British attack, so that a nuclear threat from one of them would always possess a greater inherent credibility. In such circumstances the effectiveness of British nuclear threats would depend on foreign estimates of British resolve to commit national suicide rather than give way. This estimate would surely be more influenced by an assessment of what was at stake for Britain in the dispute than by anything Britain could attempt in the way of escalation.

This brings us to the second, or political, weakness of escalation as an expedient for British governments. These are known to be actuated primarily by motives of national advantage rather than, as with the United States and Soviet Union, by ideological concepts. It is significant, for instance, that Dr. Kahn gives little or no consideration to the nature of the disputes in which the United States Government might resort to escalation. He assumes the existence of a permanent dispute in which prudence alone restrains the contestants in their mutual efforts to assert dominance. This view can be supported from the public utterances of American and Russian leaders, many of whom profess to regard themselves as engaged in an unending conflict between Good and Evil. To the extent that such ideas are sincerely held (and the events of 1967 and 1968 offer some ground for hopeful scepticism) there is an irrational element in the policies of both governments, either of which might thus be expected to pursue ideological objectives with scant regard for the outcome in terms of national advantage. The use of unlimited force by such a government is inherently credible and can be made more so by the mounting recklessness of escalation, in which each successive step tends to reinforce foreign fears that the escalating government are indeed actuated by irrational motives.

British governments, on the other hand, are widely regarded as being actuated by reasoned calculation, however faulty this may sometimes prove in practice, of the national interest. This is incompatible with national suicide and few foreigners would believe a British government capable of risking the nuclear destruction of their own nation-state except in a dispute of such gravity that giving way would entail, with equal certainty and to a corresponding degree, the destruction of the independence, the authority and the social order of Britain. Once the existence of so appalling a dilemma had lent an initial credibility to the possible British use of nuclear weapons, then a process of escalation might so reinforce the impression of British resolve as to persuade the hostile government to give way before the nuclear threshold was actually reached. No dependence, however, could be placed on so fortunate an outcome and escalation of this kind can thus be recommended only as the last resort in the most desperate of disputes.

There is, however, an analogous use of desperate force which a British government might be driven to consider. Although a sustained British escalation would probably be ineffective in any dispute not obviously involving the national existence, circumstances might arise in which a single-shot escalation could exert an advantageously catalytic effect. Britain might have committed herself so deeply in some dispute that withdrawal, though not seriously detrimental to the national interest, might nevertheless seem so humiliating as to be intolerable to national aspirations. Inadequate British forces might, for instance, have been defeated while attempting an unsuccessful defence of some British colony so distant that no counter-attack could be organized in time for limited force to reverse the *fait accompli*. A prolonged conventional war to regain the colony might have to be excluded as certain to lead to the intervention of other powers capable of frustrating British victory. Britain's own allies might be unwilling to help and British public opinion, though incensed, might be sufficiently divided to deprive any sustained attempt at escalation of the necessary minimum of credibility. In such circumstances, which are not impossibly hypothetical, what could the British Government do to alleviate the outrage to national aspirations without endangering national survival?

One answer might be a threat or act of violence sufficiently alarming to bring about the intervention of the Super-Powers without actually exposing Britain to retaliation. The United States Government cannot always be relied on to support Britain in cases involving neither American interests nor their ideological principles and the Soviet Government are even less likely to be helpful. But an act of desperate force by Britain against a third country – perhaps the spectacular, but relatively harmless, explosion of a Polaris missile off the coast or in an uninhabited area – might precipitate a crisis that would compel one or both to intervene in a manner ultimately more advantageous than mere British acquiescence. If the third country were South American, for instance, the United States might then apply pressure for a genuine compromise rather than resort to anything so drastic and unpalatable as the coercion of Britain, particularly if there were any risk of this resulting in a rapprochement between Britain and the Soviet Union. On the other hand, if the third country attracted Soviet support, this might swing the otherwise reluctant United States to the British side. Such a catalytic use of desperate force would naturally be very much of a gamble, but, if no other option were open, it would at least offer the advantage that, even if Britain ultimately had to give way, she would do so before the irresistible threats of a Super-Power and in circumstances that might deter lesser States from again provoking so dangerous a crisis.

Needless to say, none of these uses of desperate force can be recommended as the ordinary instruments of policy. If any of them has to be considered in practice, it will only be because of a failure to maintain a sufficient balance between the objectives of foreign policy and British capacities for the use of definitive or purposeful force. Unfortunately such failures have so often occurred in the course of British history that it would be unrealistic not to envisage the possibility of their repetition in the future. Moreover, the period since 1945 has seen such a change in Britain's military capacities relative to those of other countries that the employment of desperate force can no longer be considered only as the deliberate choice which, for nearly two centuries, it virtually was. This is not simply a result of the development of ballistic missiles armed with thermo-nuclear warheads: it is also due to a decline in the relative strength of the British Navy and Air Force. As long as these were capable of preventing the invasion or the effective blockade of the British Isles, any resort to desperate force by a British government remained a voluntary act. Britain was not compelled to throw down the desperate gauntlet of her guarantee to Poland in 1939. As she had chosen not to employ purposeful force at the earlier stage when this might have been effective – in repelling the German invasion of the Rhineland, for instance – Britain had nothing very obvious to gain by involving herself in European adventures and, in fact, each of her European allies proved more of a liability than an asset. When there were none left – and when British resources had been seriously depleted by a futile effort to defend other countries – Britain was still able, unaided and in spite of the pre-war neglect of her defences, to prevent invasion, to limit the effectiveness of air attack and to frustrate the submarine blockade. On purely military grounds and with all the advantages of hindsight Britain might have stood to gain from pursuing a policy of armed neutrality in the thirties and forties. Even if she had been attacked, it is arguable that an essentially defensive policy would have been as successful and much less damaging to the national interest, than the actual use of unlimited force to assert an ephemeral dominance over Germany.

These are hypothetical questions. What seems clear today is that Britain could not unaided successfully resist an attempt at invasion, at the foreign reinforcement by air or sea of an indigenous rebellion, at the blockade of the British Isles or the harassment of British shipping, without resort to desperate force. This has again been a deliberate choice, the theory apparently being that British vulnerability to nuclear attack makes it futile to incur the expenditure that an effective defence against other forms of pressure would entail. The validity of this thesis is by no means obvious. Nuclear weapons have not been employed since 1945, and, though the periodical rocket rattling of the Super-Powers may have exercised a restraining influence, actual disputes have been decided by other methods. Even the United States Government relied on a classic use of sea-power to resolve the Cuban crisis of 1962, while both Israel and North Vietnam have subsequently demonstrated the efficacy of conventional warfare even against quantitatively superior enemies.

Unfortunately, although the *use* of limited force is relatively cheap, as well as effective, the maintenance of a *capacity* for its employment is expensive. It demands enough highly trained men and modern equipment to ensure initial success in any likely trial of strength. Even the cost of naval supremacy in the Narrow Seas, together with dominance of British air-space, has seemed excessive to recent British governments, who have preferred to rely on the threat of unlimited force for their protection against all the more serious potential risks to which the independence, the authority or the social order of Britain might conceivably be exposed. This unlimited force might take three forms: a British nuclear strike, an American nuclear strike, or a conventional war fought by Britain's allies.

The restricted utility of the first has already been briefly discussed. The second, though genuinely unlimited in purely military terms, depends for its credibility on the supposed determination, in the eyes of a potential aggressor, of the British Government to invoke it and of the United States Government to apply it. As both governments would, in most foreseeable circumstances, thereby be risking the existence of their own nation-states, the effectiveness of this deterrent is at least unpredictable. The third expedient depends on the availability of American forces and the readiness of the United States Government to employ them in the defence of Britain, for it is not obvious that Britain's remaining allies would have much to spare from the defence of their own territory. American resolve would be less questionable in this case as, from their point of view, only limited force would be involved, but it is not certain that they would always have adequate capacities to spare. Nevertheless American conventional forces at present constitute Britain's principal safeguard against any threat to her vital interests by a stronger power or combination of powers.

In the short run this is naturally cheaper than the maintenance of an adequate British military capacity, but a price has nevertheless to be paid in the alignment of British policy with that of the United States Government. In certain circumstances this could involve Britain in a war which she might otherwise have wished to avoid, not least because one of the measures adopted to render American protection more credible has been the maintenance of American military bases on British soil. On the other hand, if Britain were ever to engage in a major dispute in circumstances in which she could not count on American support, the only expedient remaining would be the threat of a British nuclear strike. Paradoxically enough, therefore, the positive influence on policy of British military capacities is just the opposite of what is commonly supposed: it is not the existence of British armaments, but their inadequacy, which is most likely to result in the adoption of a dangerous foreign policy. Because post-war British governments have chosen not to pay for the defence of Britain themselves, but to rely upon the United States, they have denied themselves the option of avoiding major disputes, or terminating these by concessions, except on terms acceptable to the United States Government.

This is not the only way in which dependence on the threat of unlimited force by members of an alliance tends to result in the pursuit of more dangerous policies. Such threats are always liable to arouse scepticism if they involve one government running great risks for the sake of another or if the force envisaged is likely to invite corresponding retaliation or if the magnitude of the threat is obviously disproportionate to the issue at stake. To convince an opponent of one's potential readiness to run great risks, it thus becomes necessary actually to run minor risks and, in the interests of a fundamentally cautious policy, to display an apparent recklessness. Occasionally, as in West Berlin, there is no alternative to this trip-wire strategy: the staging of dramatic local confrontations to lend credibility to the threat of nuclear war. But it has grave disadvantages for any nation whose government is exposed to the apprehensions of a fully informed public opinion. If the military capacities of the two Super-Powers are assumed to be substatially equal in nuclear war (in the sense that they are capable of mutual destruction), the outcome of a threat of nuclear war must ultimately depend on their respective moral capacities. This is not a desirable situation for reasonable men, for the moral capacities in question are of an essentially irrational character.

History has many examples of conflicts in which a particular nation or group have achieved dominance by a manifest disregard of the ordinary pleasures of human existence. Their motives may have been rationalized under the names of honour, liberty, patriotism, religion or, more recently, ideology; disciples of Nietzsche may talk of the will to power or Freudians of the death wish: the ultimate impulse is the conviction that it is worth sacrificing the present to the future, the actual to the potential. In this sense the moral capacities of a nation are measured by the degree of disciplined recklessness in which the Government can command popular support.

Fortunately these moral capacities are not evenly distributed and appear to bear no necessary relationship to the material circumstances of the various peoples of the world. It would be inconvenient if the poorest nations were also the most aggressive and resolute. On the contrary, the achievement and preservation of the relative prosperity now enjoyed by the British people are partly attributable to the recklessness occasionally displayed by their ancestors. This has, however, often been exaggerated by popular mythology and by school historians. The assertion and maintenance of British rule in India is perhaps one of the few major instances in which the success of British foreign policy can be attributed solely to British advantage in moral capacities. Few respectable historians would nowadays contend that such great crises of British history as the Armada, Trafalgar or the Battle of Britain were decided by an inherent British advantage in courage, loyalty or discipline over their Spanish, French or German opponents. In each case the British Government of the day were able to concentrate, at the crucial point, military capacities that were at least qualitatively superior to those of their opponents. When the British Government had only recklessness on their side, they sometimes lost – as in

1066. The function, in war, of moral capacities is to tip an equal balance, or even redress an unfavourable one, but not to supply the lack of weapons or of men trained to employ them.

As instruments for the furtherance of foreign policy their utility is considerably more limited, at least for British governments. In war a degree of recklessness is acceptable, even welcome, to British public opinion and Churchill obtained a popular response in 1940 that had consistently been denied in time of peace. This is an understandable if sometimes inconvenient, distinction: once the failure of policy has compelled a resort to unlimited force, it is appropriate to run risks that would be undesirable as long as a chance remains of avoiding so desperate an expedient. In ordinary disputes, therefore, a party will always exist in Britain to urge caution, compromise, conciliation. Their public pronouncements may or may not influence the policy of the British Government, but they will certainly be noted by foreign governments and will probably influence their assessment of British resolve. In any dispute with a foreign government able to disregard the views of their own imperfectly informed public opinion, the British Government are necessarily at a disadvantage in terms of apparent moral capacities. Moreover, whereas British history books tend to emphasize the great emergencies in which the British people have displayed outstanding moral capacities, foreigners remember the more numerous occasions when British governments have backed down or given way.

This is a factor imperfectly understood in Britain, where politicians, the Press and public opinion generally tend to assume that, in matters of foreign policy, British governments mean what they say and that their utterances can command corresponding conviction and even respect abroad. On 17 March 1939, for instance, Chamberlain reacted to the German seizure of the remainder of Czechoslovakia by a speech in which he said:

'Is this the last attack upon a small State or is it to be followed by others? . . . No greater mistake could be made than to suppose that because it believes war to be a senseless and cruel thing, this nation has so lost its fibre that it will not take part to the utmost of its power in resisting such a challenge if ever it were made.'

In Britain this speech was widely regarded as signifying the end of appeasement and a major change in British policy. Even such a knowledgeable and sophisticated observer as Sir Harold Nicolson could write:

'How tremendous, for instance, must have been the effect of the Prime Minister's speech of March 17th! Those severe but simple sentences must have echoed as a gong of warning in all German hearts.'[1]

Unfortunately foreign governments are accustomed to judge the intentions of the British Government by their record and their actions rather than by their words. Neither can have inclined the German Government to take Mr. Chamberlain seriously, nor is there any reason to suppose that they were much more impressed by the subsequent guarantee to Poland on 31 March. It was on 3 April that Hitler issued his preliminary orders for the German attack on Poland (Case White) in which he assigned himself the political task of limiting the resulting war to one with Poland alone. No doubt he shared the view subsequently ascribed by Nicolson to two back-bench Tory Members of Parliament:

'I suppose we shall be able to get out of this beastly guarantee business?' 'Oh, of course. Thank God we have Neville.'[2]

When a British government threaten the use of force, foreigners ask themselves whether similar threats have

[1] Harold Nicolson, *Marginal Comment*, March Twenty-Four (Constable 1939).
[2] Harold Nicolson, *Diaries and Letters 1930–39*, op. cit., 2 May 1939.

previously been implemented, whether military preparations have been made to implement this one, whether these seem adequate to achieve the desired objective without intolerable consequences to Britain and whether the threat appears to command the general support of British public opinion. If all or most of these questions can be answered in the negative, then even the strongest and clearest and most sincerely intended words are apt to lack credibility abroad.

To this extent, therefore, it may be said that the moral capacities of the British nation have little intrinsic value as an instrument for the furtherance of foreign policy. British history testifies to their existence, but also to their intermittence. Foreign governments, being no less addicted to wishful thinking than British, are accordingly inclined to attach greater importance to the second characteristic than to the first. Unless the resolve of the British Government has been recently and consistently demonstrated in deeds rather than words, this factor will almost always be overestimated at home and undervalued abroad. In fighting a war, a British government may reasonably expect British military deficiencies to be redressed by British moral capacities: to suppose that the latter would suffice to avoid a war is the wrong kind of recklessness.

History suggests that British governments are prone to two errors in their assessment of British moral capacities. They habitually underestimate the effort and sacrifice of which the British people are capable in support of clear and consistent policies. As a result British governments fail, in time of peace, to create and maintain those capacities for the use of definitive or purposeful force which, if correctly employed, would enable disputes to be resolved without resort to the desperate force of war. They then compound their first error by exaggerating the influence on foreigners of precisely those moral capacities which they themselves have previously underestimated and thus failed to exploit in time. Moral capacities are the seed-corn of foreign policy: if cultivated in time they will promote its success; if eaten in emergency they may avert disaster, but they cannot prevent what rational men must always regard as the final failure of policy: a resort to the desperate force of war.

6

OBJECTIONS

'Whatever can be known, can be known without metaphysics, and whatever needs metaphysics for its proof cannot be proved.'

Russell[1]

HAVING now analysed the intrinsic components of British foreign policy it may be appropriate, before attempting to assemble these into a general conception or to discuss their use in the identification of disputes, to consider some of the possible objections to the line of argument so far adopted. This argument has been that the purpose of British foreign policy is to promote the independence and authority of the British nation-state, to the extent that these are compatible with preservation of the existing social order, with British national aspirations and with British national capacities. In the course of its exposition a number of detailed objections have been briefly discussed, but this argument also runs counter to certain ideas of a more fundamental character and their relevance needs to be examined before the main thesis can be pursued to any plausible conclusion.

These objections fall into three categories: the ethical, the ideological and the systematic.

The *ethical* objection is essentially to the omission, as factors liable to influence the evolution and implementation of British foreign policy, of any moral considerations independent of national interests, aspirations or capacities. Such considerations might be invoked to determine a

[1] Bertrand Russell, *Freedom and Organisation*, Chapter XVIII (Allen & Unwin 1934).

choice between conflicting components of the national interest, or to tip the balance when interests and aspirations appear to indicate different courses or, in the most extreme case, to reject or modify a policy that met the requirements alike of natural interests, aspirations and capacities. So far, for instance, there has been a tendency to regard the national interest (and, within the national interest, the elements of independence and authority) as making the most positive contribution to the formation of policy, whereas maintenance of the existing social order, national aspirations and national capacities have been considered primarily as limiting factors. Are there any moral principles which would confirm or refute such a preference? Alternatively, whatever the relative values accorded to interests, aspirations and capacities, do there exist moral principles which British governments can be expected to prefer to all three?

These are difficult questions. On the one hand, British governments almost always invoke moral principles in support either of their policy or of the expedients chosen for its implementation. On the other hand, the validity of their arguments is invariably challenged, sometimes with a degree of plausibility, either by their domestic opponents or by foreigners. The human inability of British governments invariably to practise what they preach need not detain us: what matters is whether there actually are identifiable moral doctrines capable of clear distinction from the interests of the British nation-state or the aspirations of the British people. This problem is treated at length by Professor Carr in his classic work, *The Twenty Years' Crisis*, and it is hard to dissent from his view that:

> 'Theories of social morality are always the product of a dominant group which identifies itself with the community as a whole and which possesses facilities denied to subordinate groups or individuals for imposing its view of life on the community. Theories of international morality are, for the same reason and in

virtue of the same process, the product of dominant nations or groups of nations.'

'. . . these supposedly absolute and universal principles were not principles at all, but the unconscious reflexions of national policy based on a particular interpretation of national interest at a particular time. There is a sense in which peace and co-operation between nations or classes or individuals is a common and universal end irrespective of conflicting interests and politics. There is a sense in which a common interest exists in the maintenance of order, whether it be international order or "law and order" within the nation. But as soon as the attempt is made to apply these supposedly abstract principles to a concrete political situation, they are revealed as the transparent disguises of selfish vested interests. The bankruptcy of utopianism resides not in its failure to live up to its principles, but in the exposure of its inability to provide any absolute and disinterested standard for the conduct of international affairs.'[1]

Professor Carr, of course, was primarily concerned with the ideas of international morality prevalent in Britain and the United States before 1939, but his insistence on an 'absolute and disinterested standard' provides a criterion equally applicable today. This is a practical test, not a metaphysical one. Moral precepts are useful when they command sufficient acceptance within a given environment to offer a reliable short-cut to decisions. In Britain, for instance, it is generally accepted as being wrong for one man to kill another. This greatly simplifies the task of the Government and administration: they do not have to consider whether or on what grounds it might be argued that the victim was better dead. Killing him fell into a class of actions regarded as wrong in almost all circumstances in which they were deliberately committed. This principle, however, would lose its practical utility if it admitted of large and ill-defined exceptions, if persons of Welsh ancestry were legitimate victims or if ministers of

[1] E. H. Carr, *The Twenty Years' Crisis*, op. cit., Chapter 5.

religion were allowed to kill sinners. The immorality of killing would then no longer constitute a reliable and sufficient guide to decisions, nor would this principle be accepted by Welshmen and sinners as even approximating to an absolute and disinterested standard. Each case of murder would then have to be judged on other considerations and it is likely that all concerned would be guided by an assessment of their respective interests, aspirations and capacities.

Such an assessment is always complex and it would undoubtedly be convenient if, within the larger international environment, there existed a class of actions generally accepted as wrong whoever committed them and whatever the circumstances. It might then become a precept that the British Government should invariably avoid taking such actions and should condemn them when taken by other nation-states. If there also existed some international organization able and willing effectively to discourage nation-states from committing these actions, thereby reducing violations of international morality to the same relatively insignificant proportion as murders in civilized states, it would be worth the while of the British Government to accept some sacrifice of British interests and aspirations in individual cases in order to uphold the general rule. But, if it is admitted that a particular kind of action may be 'wrong' when taken by one state in one set of circumstances, yet 'right' when taken by another in different circumstances, then the moral principle involved lacks sufficient certainty to constitute a reliable guide to decision or to override the arguments of interest, aspiration and capacity. It would take a separate book adequately to support the proposition that all the ideas of international morality now current are of this relative, partial and uncertain kind, but a few examples may help to illustrate an assertion already argued by other authors.

For instance, one of the most popular and seemingly

unassailable of contemporary moral ideas is that 'peace' is better than war. Scarcely anyone, however, regards this as an absolute standard. Most people in Britain probably consider 'peace' as inseparable from the maintenance of a *status quo* that confers on them a standard of living much above the average enjoyed by the human race. Although they might think it 'wrong' for Britain to go to war merely to increase her present advantage over other countries, they would probably consider it 'right' for her to use even desperate force against invasion, foreign domination, the threat of starvation or any other really grave interference by a foreign government with 'our way of life'. In brief, while agreeing with Mr. Macmillan that 'peace is the supreme purpose of all policy',[1] they would make an exception for the right of 'self-defence' against 'aggression'.

But what is 'aggression'? Ever since 1945 the United Nations have been trying, so far in vain, to agree on a definition and, whenever an actual war takes place, it is customary for both sides to claim to be the victims of aggression, to put forward plausible arguments in support of their proposition and to be upheld in these arguments by third parties. Is the aggressor the nation to fire the first shot or the nation to make the first threatening move? If the former, must the shot be fired by a member of the regular armed forces or is it enough if an act of violence is committed with the connivance of the supposedly aggressor State? What constitutes a threatening move? There is no end to such questions, but most governments – the British not least – have in practice tended to answer them on political or military grounds and to produce their moral justification afterwards. Few people in Britain, for instance, would be likely to approve of a British government which, having witnessed the mobilization and deployment of hostile forces, risked defeat by deferring their action until the enemy was quite ready to fire the first shot.

[1] See Chapter 2.

Indeed, British enthusiasts for 'peace' sometimes seem to concentrate mainly on those issues where peace can be preserved or restored by sacrifices on the part of foreigners, particularly such foreigners as engage in 'a quarrel in a far-away country of which we know nothing'.[1]

During the sixties, for instance, there was considerable popular support for 'peace in Vietnam', an objective which, it was suggested, could be attained by concessions on the part of the United States Government and a section of the Vietnamese people. The political merits and feasibility of this idea need not be discussed here, but it should be noted that the sacrifices involved were all to be made by foreigners, whereas one of the advantages – eliminating the risk that this particular conflict might escalate into general war – would benefit the British people. A pure pacifist might argue that any sacrifice should be accepted rather than prolong a war, but how can any British subject willing, in certain circumstances, to fight for his own country, maintain, as a moral rather than a political principle, that foreigners are wrong to do the same?

Other arguments are accordingly invoked to justify the proposition that this is a moral issue. The idea that the South Vietnamese Government are morally in the wrong because some of their members or supporters have committed acts normally regarded as wrong in private individuals in Britain need not detain us. All governments, including all British governments, commit or encourage in time of war actions capable of being described as immoral. Nor is it morally, as opposed to politically, relevant that some of the inhabitants of South Vietnam are opposed to their Government and others are at best indifferent. This applies to almost all countries on whose territory a war is being waged.

There are, however, two more serious propositions:

[1] Broadcast by Mr. Chamberlain about Czechoslovakia on 27 September 1938.

that the objectives of the North Vietnamese are morally 'right' or, alternatively, that any foreign government participating in a conflict among Vietnamese is morally 'wrong'.

The first proposition rests on the assumption that the North Vietnamese are endeavouring to complete the process of national liberation and that anyone opposing them in this endeavour can accordingly be equated with the former colonial power. This brings into play the well-known principle that:

> 'The national liberation war of a dependent people against a colonial power will always be a just, defensive war, both from the political and from the legal point of view, irrespective of who started military operations . . .'[1]

Unfortunately the application of this principle (whatever its intrinsic merits) to Vietnam requires a fairly broad definition of the phrase 'colonial power' which, if it is to possess moral validity, must be shown to constitute an absolute standard capable of general application. This is not, however, the view even of the Soviet Government. As Mr. Khruschev had earlier told the *New York Times*:

> 'The situation in Hungary is absolutely different, for Hungary is an independent State with its own independent Government and pursues its own policy.'[2]

Yet, if a government in Hungary had the right in 1956 to summon twelve Soviet armoured divisions to overthrow another Hungarian Government and to suppress the resistance of one section of the Hungarian people, how can the government in Saigon, who proved by fighting alone for some years that they enjoyed the support of at least some of their people, be denied a similar right to seek American assistance? By what 'absolute and disinterested standard' can it be said that Mr. Ho Chi Minh

[1] *Soviet State and Law*, No. 10 of October 1957.
[2] *New York Times*, 10 May 1957.

is a national liberator, but that Mr. Imre Nagy was not; that the United States have a colonial rôle in Vietnam, but that the Soviet Union did not in Hungary? And, if the Vietnamese themselves disagree on what constitutes their own liberation, what moral right has any foreigner to decide the issue for them?

This manifest division of the Vietnamese people, though it destroys the idea of a war of national liberation, is itself invoked by supporters of the second proposition: that 'all nations must have the freedom to arrange their own national life' and that 'no Power shall interfere in the struggle of any other nation to change its ideology'.[1]

This proposition implies that it is 'right' for the Vietnamese themselves to decide by civil war the future pattern of their national life and ideology, but 'wrong' for foreign governments to take any part in the struggle. As with any other moral principle, the most appropriate test of its absolute and disinterested character is to inquire whether those who support it apply the same standard to their own conduct. This particular principle was propounded by Mr. Sukarno, then President of Indonesia, who subsequently sent his troops into Malaysia and later fell from power after an unsuccessful attempt to change the ideology of his own country with Chinese assistance. Among his supporters at the Belgrade Conference were representatives of the Egyptian and Saudi Arabian Governments who subsequently intervened on opposite sides in the civil war in the Yemen. Even persons uncorrupted by the responsibilities of power tend to modify their condemnation of interference in the internal affairs of another State if they happen to disapprove of its government. Many of those most opposed to American intervention in Vietnam have simultaneously advocated British intervention in Rhodesia or even in Greece.

Naturally the advocates of international morality share

[1] Proceedings of the Belgrade Conference of Non-Aligned Countries 1961.

the capacity of other casuists to explain the diverse application of their principles. It may thus be argued that non-intervention would be right in Vietnam because it would help to end the bad state of war, but that it would be wrong in Greece or Rhodesia because it would help to perpetuate the rule of a bad government. But once the moral test is shifted from the nature of actions to their results, the element of simplicity and certainty is lost. Almost all actions benefit some people and harm others. It accordingly becomes necessary to prefer the good of one group to the misfortune of another. But, if such a choice is to be made, it is not obvious that any group can have a better claim on the British Government than their own people or that there exist any moral considerations of greater significance to British foreign policy than British national interests and aspirations.

It may nevertheless be argued that moral ideas, however dubious their philosophical basis and however relative and partial their practical application, are believed by many human beings to exist and to exercise intermittent influence on their private behaviour. May this not also be true of governments, so that moral considerations, however imperfect or hypocritical, nevertheless influence policy in the form of doctrines that have acquired an effective value independent of their truth? We have already noted that the political doctrine of 'early resistance to aggressive dictators', which Lord Avon had evolved in the thirties, influenced British policy in 1956. It might similarly be contended that a moral doctrine – the condemnation of aggressive war (however ambiguous this may be) – was responsible for the elaborate pretence that the British and French forces which attacked Egypt were only engaged in separating the combatants in an entirely fortuitous war between Israel and Egypt. If it is argued that a moral doctrine, rather than considerations of political expediency, was paramount, this contention requires the assumption that the British Government initially regarded an attack on Egypt as morally wrong. If so, it would not have been inconsistent with the ordinary standards of conduct among private individuals priding themselves on their morality for the British Government so to have contrived matters that this burden was lifted from their conscience by fresh developments. On the evidence so far available, however, there is little to suggest that British Ministers regarded the use of force against Egypt as morally wrong at any stage after the nationalization of the Suez Canal Company. If they preferred to delay this until after the outbreak of war between Israel and Egypt, their motive seems primarily to have been to appease the opposition, both domestic and international, that had arisen during the months allowed to elapse since Lord Avon had telegraphed, on 27 July 1956, to President Eisenhower:

> 'My colleagues and I are convinced that we must be ready, in the last resort, to use force to bring Nasser to his senses.'[1]

Nor was this opposition exclusively, or even primarily, based on any moral abhorrence of the use of force to counter Egyptian policy. At the outset both Mr. Dulles and Mr. Gaitskell had employed the language of moral condemnation in an opposite sense, the former talking of the need 'to make Nasser disgorge', the latter comparing him to Hitler and Mussolini. Both had then accepted the possible use of force on certain conditions. For Dulles this entailed creating 'a world opinion so adverse to Nasser that he would be isolated',[2] for Gaitskell 'circumstances . . . consistent with our belief in, and our pledges to the Charter of the United Nations'.[3] Both stipulations might have been expedient, but it is hard to consider them moral: if ethical absolutes exist and there is any significance in describing the use of force against Egypt as either

[1] Anthony Eden, *Full Circle*, op. cit., Book III, Chapter I.
[2] Anthony Eden, ibid.
[3] *Hansard*, 2 August 1956.

'right' or 'wrong', then it was irrelevant whether or not Nasser was isolated or whether or not British action could be represented as consistent with the Charter of the United Nations. These were political arguments, which might have been construed as an invitation to provide a pretext for the use of force rather than as a warning against its employment. Indeed, it is arguable that, if British military capacities had permitted the use of immediate force against Egypt and if this had resulted in a rapid military victory, many of those later foremost in censure would have been the first to applaud. Whether such a victory would have altered the policy or composition of the Egyptian Government or advanced British interests is, of course, quite another matter. But the actual course of events scarcely suggests that any of those involved were primarily actuated by moral considerations of an absolute and disinterested character.

Nevertheless the British Government did go to considerable trouble to invest their military action with a moral cloak, even if this subsequently proved so threadbare as to become the chief target of their critics. Nor was the Suez Crisis the only occasion on which British governments have acted as if they believed the British people to hold moral views with which foreign policy, however arrived at, needed to be reconciled. Mr. Woodhouse's question[1] – 'which policy is morally right?' – may be strictly unanswerable, but British politicians still consider it worth asking, however disingenuous some of their own replies may occasionally seem. Ought it not, therefore, to be included among the factors that go to make up British foreign policy, even if only in the revised form of: 'which policy will British public opinion consider morally right?'

Such a question would have the attraction of being simpler and more familiar than the somewhat cumbrous process suggested in Chapter 2 for the ascertainment of

[1] See Chapter 2.

national aspirations. Moreover, whatever arguments may be advanced here, this question is going to be asked and answered. It is so much easier to discuss problems and decisions in terms of 'right' and 'wrong', 'bad' and 'good', that neither individuals nor governments will readily relinquish such a convenient short-cut to persuasion. To proclaim a particular policy 'morally right' is not necessarily a less defensible compression of the argument than to say that it is 'in the national interest' and it would be neither intellectually justifiable nor practically useful to attempt to discourage the use of such language merely on the grounds that it is meaningless. Politicians have to persuade people to do things and must be allowed to employ the type of exhortation which experience has led them to consider most effective. The danger is not that they will deceive the people – some degree of deception is inevitable in the communication of imperfectly comprehended ideas – but that they will deceive themselves.

Moral ideas undoubtedly exist and their metaphysical validity is largely irrelevant to their political influence. But they are by no means the only component of national aspirations, nor does every sincerely held moral opinion necessarily constitute a valid national aspiration. There are many things which the British people either want or do not want for which even the most wishful imagination could not assign a moral motive. And British public opinion may genuinely consider a particular policy morally right without being prepared to pay for its consequences. Collectively no less than individually, the British people draw a tacit distinction between what is 'right' and what is 'practical'. And it is much more important for governments to know which policy the people will support than which sentiments they will applaud. Yet if a policy is presented for popular endorsement as a straightforward moral issue, there may be a misleading reluctance on the part of the public to declare their opposition. Most people prefer to be 'against sin' until the arrival of the bill for good works. Moreover, even if this reluctance is expressed, the politician may find it harder to detect if he has meanwhile committed himself to a firm moral view. If one wants an accurate answer it is preferable to ask a precise question.

It is not, however, in public debate that the greatest, and most easily avoidable, danger of the moral approach to foreign policy is to be found. Speakers and audience alike always make allowance for the licence of oratory. The true risk attaches to those private discussions in which policy is actually decided. If these have been rationally conducted, then the public use of moral arguments to justify decisions reached on other grounds may be defensible as the most convenient method of reconciling policy with national aspirations. But, if the original decision was actually taken on moral grounds, then it is likely to have been reached under the influence of emotion rather than of reason. Moral ideas not only spring from emotion: they also generate it. The more successfully, therefore, that a moral idea is advanced as a pretext for action, the greater the risk that this idea will acquire an influence of its own, so that the policy becomes the creature of emotion and ceases to be susceptible of rational control and modification. A moral doctrine has the same dangerous characteristic as a political doctrine: it tends to outlast the particular combination of circumstances that gave it birth. But its obsolescence is much more difficult to establish by reasoned argument. It is one thing to say that a particular course of action has ceased, owing to unforeseen developments, to be advantageous: it is much more difficult to argue that what was once 'right' has now become 'wrong'.

During the Suez Crisis, for instance, there was one moral idea which, whatever may be thought of its intrinsic validity, undoubtedly did influence the British Government. This was that President Nasser's nationalization of the Suez Canal Company constituted an act of 'theft'. If Lord Avon had been less fervently and lastingly[1] seized of this moral conviction, he might have found it easier to make, and to enlist the assistance of others in making, a more dispassionate assessment of the course of action indicated by British interests, aspirations and capacities. If Nasser was merely a foreign leader inimical to British interests, then British policy towards him could be determined by calculating the degree of advantage offered by different courses of action, a coolness of choice excluded by the conviction that he was a 'megalomaniacal dictator' with his 'thumb on our windpipe'. Moreover, if this was a contest between good and evil, it could be argued that the vacillations of American policy were irrelevant: what was morally right in July, when Mr. Dulles wanted 'to make Nasser disgorge' did not cease to be right in October merely because Mr. Dulles had meanwhile changed his mind and uttered his celebrated warning that the United States would be 'playing a somewhat independent role'.[2] Morality, no less than love, is not morality 'which alters when it alteration finds'. Policy, however, needs to be more flexible.

There is one final reason for preferring national aspirations to morality as a criterion for the formulation and exposition of foreign policy. This is that the moral arguments of British politicians are often so profoundly irritating to foreigners as to constitute a serious impediment to the peaceful resolution of disputes. It is not only foreign susceptibilities which make it easier for a British government to reach agreement by calling for a mutually advantageous reconciliation of conflicting interests rather than for foreign recognition that their cause is 'wrong' and that of the British Government 'right'. It often happens that the foreign government have moral doctrines of their own and that these, whatever their validity or sincerity,

[1] Three years later he chose 'Theft' as the title of the chapter describing this episode in his memoirs, *Full Circle*.

[2] All the preceding quotations are from: Anthony Eden, op. cit.

differ so fundamentally from those of the British Government that any moral dialogue becomes impossible for want of a common language in which to conduct it. This is one of the causes of the so-called 'double standard' of international morality, which excites such indignation in some British politicians. Interest, on the other hand, is as international a dialect as money or power and is better adapted to the promotion of understanding among the nations of the world.

It is thus on grounds of practical expediency that the reader is invited to reject moral considerations as an appropriate influence on the formation and evolution of British foreign policy. Anyone with greater faith than Lord Russell in the value of metaphysics may like, however, also to consider the following proposition, which is submitted with all the humility required of amateur excursions into that difficult field. The nation-state exists and, as with other living entities, its primary purpose is to continue existing. This purpose cannot be achieved without the maintenance of its independence and authority. The attainment of these objectives is subject to the limiting factors discussed earlier. National capacities might prove inadequate to the task or this might entail a transformation of the social order incompatible with national aspirations or with the continued identity of the nation-state. Within these broad limits, however, it is difficult to conceive of any moral imperative that could override, for a British government, the objective of national self-preservation or to suggest methods of attaining this objective more efficacious than those of reasoned analysis and decision.

The *ideological* objection is that foreign policy should have a more positive purpose than the mere preservation of the nation-state. The alternatives suggested are remarkably various, but those capable of influencing governments fall into two broad categories. There are the theories which, while accepting that the continued existence of the nation-state is desirable, attach more importance to the nature of its social order than to its independence and authority. And there are the theories which regard the nation-state as no more than the instrument of a wider purpose. The first type of theorist may consider it more important for Britain to be democratic or socialist or Christian or devoted to private enterprise than to maintain or increase the existing level of her independence and external authority. If he also expects the British Government to promote his preferred variety of social order in foreign countries as well, he is approaching the views of the second type of theorist, to whom the national identity of Britain is secondary to the progress throughout the world of his chosen ideology. Such objectors do not, of course, contend that British governments are in fact habitually prompted by ideological motives, only that they ought to be.

There is naturally no dispute about the influence of the social order on foreign policy. It helps to determine the prevailing conception of national interests, aspirations and capacities. Changes in the social order are thus automatically reflected both in the ends assigned to foreign policy and in the resources available for its execution. Nor is it only actual changes in the social order which modify foreign policy. A different attitude on the part of the British Government, an increased emphasis either on stability or on change, cannot be confined to domestic affairs, but has inevitable repercussions abroad as well. 'Conservative foreign policy' or 'Socialist foreign policy' may be difficult ideas to define in terms that would command the assent of most Conservatives or of most Socialists, but, in so far as the domestic policies of these two parties are different, then these differences are bound to be reflected in their foreign policies as well. Even if a new government have no conscious intention of modifying the foreign policy of their predecessors, their domestic decisions are likely to have this result. A Conservative government could not, for instance, reduce taxation, or a Socialist government increase welfare expenditure, without affecting the resources available to support the objectives of foreign policy.

Many theorists, whether of the Left or of the Right, would nevertheless argue that the differences between the foreign policies of one British Government and another are insufficiently clear-cut and consistent. Many of the important decisions taken since 1945 in the field of foreign policy were denounced by the Opposition of the time, only to be tacitly accepted when that Opposition came to power. Sometimes, as in the case of British withdrawal from India, this decision may have been beyond the power of the next government to reverse, but it would not have been impossible for a Labour Foreign Secretary to have adopted in 1964 a policy towards Vietnam fundamentally different from that of his Conservative predecessor. The objection advanced by such theorists is that the omission from our definition of foreign policy of any ideological criteria tends to perpetuate a state of affairs in which, but for minor variations and shades of emphasis, British foreign policy evolves on lines largely independent of democratic control or of the opinions expressed at successive general elections. To their mind a government with a radically different conception of the social order should also have a radically different conception of foreign policy.

This is an arguable theory, but it ignores two inconvenient facts. The first is that British governments during the twentieth century have not, for all the sound and fury of British politicians, actually manifested any very fundamental difference in their attitudes towards the social order. When in opposition the leaders of each party attack most of the domestic decisions taken by the Government of the day, but these decisions are seldom disturbed when the opposition themselves come to power. The basic continuity of foreign policy merely reflects a similar phenomenon in domestic policy. Moreover, even if Conservative and Socialist conceptions of the desirable social order in Britain were more divergent than they are, it is unlikely that either party, when in power, would wish to see any significant reduction in the British standard of living or in the ability of the British Government to give effect to their own views on the evolution of the British social order. Indeed, the more ardently a British politician desires to preserve, or to transform, the British social order, the more important it becomes to him to be able to do so without foreign interference or obstruction. Whatever his views in opposition, therefore, the importance of maintaining national independence and authority soon becomes evident to the politician in power. This does not mean that every politician interprets the three concepts of independence, authority and the social order similarly, or that the relative value attached to each never differs. Numerous examples to the contrary have been quoted in earlier chapters. But governments, unlike backbenchers, cannot avoid considering all three factors in the evolution of their foreign policy as long as they wish to preserve the nation-state and their own power to influence events.

This is largely due to the second inconvenient fact: the existence of foreigners. Although some Englishmen seem to find this as difficult to believe in as the difference of the sexes, foreign States do exist. They have their own customs, their own interests, their own aspirations and their own sense of identity. They do not attach the same importance as British politicians to the results of British general elections nor do they always regard these as sufficient reason for modifying their own policies or their attitude towards the British Government. Although a new British Foreign Secretary may sincerely desire to make radical alterations in his predecessor's policy, he may thus find that foreign governments will not adapt themselves to his views and that, being confronted with substantially the same problems, he is unable to avoid substantially similar responses.

The limitations imposed on British policy by the existence of foreigners are more fully considered in the next chapter, but there is one factor which is immediately relevant to the concept of ideological objectives. There is at present no conceivable social order for Britain which could relieve the British people from their dependence on imports for most of their food and raw materials. These imports would not be forthcoming – and the British people would starve – without the acquiescence of foreign governments. To preserve the livelihood of the British people it is accordingly necessary for any British Government to secure this minimum of foreign acquiescence, whether by conciliation or by coercion. Either course may and, in practice, often does, require the British Government to depart from the purity of any ideological doctrine they may profess. The more responsive the British Government are to the wishes of the people, the greater the concessions that have to be made to expediency. This is a consideration particularly applicable to the idea that British relations with foreign States should be determined by the extent to which their social order either resembles or differs from that preferred by the British Government of the day. Even in the rare cases when British interests are not directly involved, this is a difficult standard to apply, because foreign institutions are seldom simply comparable with those of Britain. But, all too often, the maintenance (let alone the improvement) of the social order in Britain demands the toleration of a very different state of affairs abroad. In practice this toleration is forthcoming not only to preserve for the British people the basic necessities of life, but also their luxuries: tobacco, foreign films, holidays on the Costa Brava, sherry, petrol for private motoring, annual wage increases. When it comes to sacrificing luxuries, the first to go is usually the ideological conscience of the British Government and it would be an unusual politician who maintained that his electors would demand a different choice.

This is not, of course, a dilemma which confronts the second school of ideological objectors, who are fully prepared to sacrifice, not only the independence and authority of the nation-state, but also the material welfare of the British people. At all stages of our history there have been Britons eager to urge the superior claims of Christendom, of the Holy Catholic Church, of the Protestant Cause, of Liberty, of Democracy, of Communism or of anti-Communism. Cardinal Allen, having explained why Queen Elizabeth I had forfeited all claim to allegiance, exhorted Englishmen to serve King Philip of Spain in order:

> 'to reduce our people to the obedience of Christ's Church and deliver our Catholic friends and brethren from the damnable and intolerable yoke of heresy.'[1]

He would have understood – and some of his twentieth-century compatriots would have echoed – Mr. Kádár's flat declaration:

> 'No man living in any country can call himself progressive, unless he is loyal to the U.S.S.R.'[2]

These two contrasting ideologists, the English Catholic exile and the Hungarian Quisling, illustrate one of the basic weaknesses of such arguments: in practice and in any particular case they nearly always tend to require the sacrifice of British national interests to those of another nation-state. It is thus difficult to regard them as possessing a character any more absolute or disinterested than the moral arguments earlier considered. Their apologists, of course, contend that this consequence of their arguments is purely coincidental: at any given time another government may be the standard-bearer of the particular ideology

[1] Quoted in Garrett Mattingley, *The Defeat of the Spanish Armada*, Chapter VI (Jonathan Cape 1959).

[2] *Népszabadság*, 29 January 1958.

in question, but this does not detract from its intrinsic validity or its ultimate value to the British people not, perhaps, as such, but as part of the human race. This is not an argument which, at least since 1688, appears to have commended itself to the British people, who have generally taken the view that, bad though British governments habitually are, a foreign government would be even worse.

Even where the ideology concerned does not require any immediate sacrifice of the authority and independence of the British nation-state, some scepticism is still permissible. There are so many of these ideologies, their permutations are so various and their fluctuations so frequent, that it would be intolerably tedious to analyse them all, not least because some will have disappeared and others emerged before even this book is out of print. It is thus tempting to rely on the historical argument. Since at least the twelfth century England has been an identifiable entity, which was enlarged and fortified, but not altered in any essential particular, by the subsequent Union with Scotland. During the years that have followed the social order has changed out of all recognition as have the ideologies that continue to torment the human race. What is Christendom now, where is the 'Free World', which is Communism? But the principle of nationality, the general recognition of a clear distinction between one nation and another, has not merely survived while institutions have crumbled and ideologies withered: it has actually acquired new strength with the passage of time. Nationalism during the twentieth century has exerted more influence, and all the ideologies less, both on British governments and on British public opinion, than in most earlier periods of our history.

Nor is this entirely a British idiosyncrasy or even one confined to long established and traditionally minded nation-states. The unprecedented rate at which new States have emerged during recent years, no less than the slender claim of some of them to any prior nationhood, makes it premature to risk any general judgement on the relative ascendancy of nationality or ideology in the world as a whole. Nevertheless, of the seventy odd new States created since 1918, more have undergone violent transformation of their social order and ideology (sometimes more than once) than have disintegrated or vanished from the map. This is not necessarily a permanent tendency and it remains conceivable that some new ideology will eventually arise and, for a time, sweep all before it. In 1968, however, nationalism appears to be the most potent influence on the majority of governments and, in Britain at least, has enjoyed this dominant rôle more often and for longer periods than any other. It may thus be argued that all ideologies are ephemeral and that none of them are as integral to the existence of a nation-state and its Government as the concepts of national independence and authority.

The arguments for rejecting ideology as a direct influence on British foreign policy are thus that the British Government need independence and authority if they are to determine the kind of social order that shall prevail in Britain; that no conceivable kind of social order can be maintained without a readiness to compromise with those foreign governments that cannot be coerced; and that no ideology has yet manifested the same consistence, the same relevance or so durable an appeal to the British people as the combination of interest and sentiment that goes to make up nationalism. Ideological considerations, no less than moral, must thus be regarded as merely a potential component of national aspirations, through which they may indirectly influence foreign policy to the extent that they are compatible with national interests and capacities.

The ethical and ideological objections are, however, incidental: they call for the addition of new components to the general conception of British foreign policy without necessarily invalidating the arguments on which this has been erected. The *systematic* objection is much more fundamental and, in various forms, far more current among contemporary students of international affairs. It has been stated with force and clarity by Mr. Burton, the Senior Lecturer in International Relations at the University College in London:

'International Relations is concerned, amongst other things, with all events and situations affecting more than one State. In a deductive approach to politics it is customary to make references to past situations and events by way of example, and in an inductive approach, by way of support for a theory. In either case there is reference to history and to current affairs. In both cases the reference has value only if, first the record of events is exact and, second, there is agreement on the interpretation of the record.

'Herein lies one of the major obstacles to a consensus in International Relations. It is not difficult to give examples in support of a preconceived theory, no matter how improbable, and it is easy to extract from the record sufficient evidence on which to build any theory. Even the most objective and scientific of students will be misled by reference to the historical or current record of particular events. In one's own experience there are many situations in which one has had direct participation, and about the details of which one believes one is clear; yet the Press and the texts report quite differently. The latter may be correct – they may reflect a better perspective than an actor could have; but one questions the usefulness of references to particular happenings to demonstrate or to support a theory when widely different recordings and interpretations of fact are possible. One may take aspects of the Suez, Cuban or Dutch-Indonesian disputes to prove almost any proposition one wishes to argue; the facts and their interpretation can be arranged accordingly. It is still more misleading, probably, to take events and situations that are beyond living memory. Furthermore, apart from difficulties of fact and interpretation related to a particular situation, there is an infinite number of cases in the history of man from which to select, and reference to a small number of them cannot be regarded as a reliable basis for generalization.'[1]

[1] J. W. Burton, *International Relations – A General Theory*, Chapter I. (Cambridge University Press 1965).

It is difficult to imagine a more comprehensive, a more pointed or a more damning indictment of the entire system of argument adopted in the present work. Before abandoning this in despair as, for similar reasons, Sir Walter Raleigh is said to have abandoned his 'History of the World', it may be as well to examine the alternative approaches favoured by this and other academic authorities. In doing so it will be important to bear in mind the purpose of the present work: to suggest the kind of theoretical questions to be asked by those confronted by the practical problems of British foreign policy. This is a rather different objective from the academic search for general principles of unassailable validity. Although it remains desirable that any arguments employed should have a demonstrably sound basis, it is no less important that this basis should be closely related to the conclusion it is intended to support and that the intervening arguments should be of a character acceptable to their audience. If the fundamental axiom is too remote, then the advantages of its added validity will be lost in the elaborate chain of argument (with its consequential possibilities of error) needed to relate it to the final precept.

For instance, of all the propositions devised by human intelligence, the least vulnerable to the objections of common sense is probably the famous *cogito ergo sum* – I think, therefore I exist. But even the great Descartes himself went sadly astray when he attempted to make further deductions from this admirable premise. In less expert hands the shorter the reasoning, the less the likelihood of error, even if the initial premise has, at best, only a restricted and particular claim to validity. The motorist whose car has broken down may find it more useful to know how another motorist solved a similar problem – however imperfectly or inaccurately that problem is described – than to receive a lecture on the principles of the internal combustion engine. He may also prefer this advice to be conveyed in the kind of language with which he is already familiar, even if this involves a degree of approximation and imprecision. There are thus three tests to which any alternative approach to the theory of British foreign policy should be submitted: are the initial assumptions valid; are they closely related to the conclusions they support; and are the concepts and terms employed in argument likely to be acceptable to British politicians and officials?

Mr. Burton's first alternative, for instance, is to base his arguments on:

> 'Observable long-term trends which appear consistent, and on which one might reliably predict. Population growth, improvement in communications, decreasing illiteracy, increasing destructive power of weapons, and the progressive development of the modern State towards centralization, and less certainly, increasing nationalism and resistance to foreign domination, may be regarded as trends.'[1]

Superficially this is an attractive argument. To anyone looking backwards from 1968 the existence of such trends might appear more obvious and a better basis for theory than the sometimes conflicting historical accounts of particular events. Unfortunately most long-term trends are subject to discontinuities in particular periods or particular places. In Britain, for instance, there have been periods in which population has fallen[2] or communications have deteriorated. A trend may thus be true in the long term but false for the immediate period or the particular area in which decisions must be taken. This weakness becomes even more evident when secondary predictions are based on even a genuine trend. At the beginning of the nineteenth century, for instance, Malthus correctly observed the existence of a long-term trend towards the growth of population in Europe. But his

[1] J. W. Burton, op. cit.

[2] This has not happened throughout the entire country for centuries, but the population of Scotland was declining in the nineteen sixties and this trend was expected to continue.

secondary prediction that this would rapidly outstrip Europe's ability to feed her inhabitants and his contemptuous rejection of 'the wildness of speculation . . . (of course more in jest than in earnest) that Europe should grow its corn in America' have so far proved seriously misleading. Moreover, when it came to offering practical advice to counter the disasters he foresaw, his advocacy of 'moral restraint' suggests that his process of reasoning might have benefited considerably from a more liberal use of 'reference to particular happenings'. Some twenty years before these gloomy predictions an English historian had paused in his voluminous record of particular happenings fifteen centuries earlier to reflect upon their lessons for the future. In one of the great passages of English prose he argued convincingly that:

> 'We may therefore acquiesce in the pleasing conclusion, that every age of the world has increased, and still increases, the real wealth, the happiness, the knowledge, and perhaps the virtue, of the human race.'[1]

In 1968 his prophecies have yet to be proved wrong, but the discernment of these great trends in human history can have been of singularly little assistance to the British statesmen who had, a dozen years later, to grapple with the disruption of what then seemed European civilization by the French Revolution and the Napoleonic Wars. Myopia is not the only defect to which human vision is liable and history does not suggest that international historical trends have so far furnished a basis for prediction, for theory or for practical advice so much more reliable as to outweigh the greater difficulty of relating them to immediate problems.

Another alternative offered by Mr. Burton is:

> 'to argue on the basis of a hypothetical situation using symbols for States, and stating the circumstances.'[2]

[1] Edward Gibbon, *Decline and Fall of the Roman Empire*, Chapter 38 (Chatto & Windus 1875).

[2] J. W. Burton, op. cit.

Although it is far from obvious how this method makes it any more

> 'difficult to give examples in support of a preconceived theory, no matter how improbable'.[1]

This quasi-scientific approach was very fashionable during the sixties, when games theory and other mathematical concepts were invoked to explain international relations in ostensibly objective terms. The attractions of this approach are obvious, but so are its pitfalls. A theorem is even more remote from the practical problems of everyday life than a historical trend and the possibilities of error in the intervening argument are correspondingly greater. Even in the supposedly more reliable domain of the sciences sometimes called exact it can be extremely dangerous to make secondary predictions. In 1933, for instance, one of the greatest and most far-seeing of British physicists declared:

> 'These transformations of the atom are of extraordinary interest to scientists, but we cannot control nuclear energy to an extent which would be of any value commercially, and I believe we are not likely ever to be able to do so.'[2]

When Lord Rutherford thus erred, he was straying only a little beyond the sphere in which he had achieved unquestioned authority. The dangers of applying to international relations even the most plausible analogies drawn from anthropology, cybernetics or zoology are even more obvious. But the real objection to the quasi-scientific approach to international relations can only be appreciated by those who have studied some of the results, particularly in recent American writings. Here is an example from Professor Boulding of the University of Michigan:

[1] J. W. Burton, op. cit.

[2] Lord Rutherford, quoted in C. P. Snow, *Variety of Men* (Macmillan 1967).

> 'In order to bring together the variables associated with each nation or pair of nations in the international system, we must resort to the device of a matrix, as in Figure 1. Here the hostility-friendliness variable is used as an example. Each cell a_{ij} indicates the degree of hostility or friendliness of nation I (of the row) towards nation J (of the column). For purposes of illustration, arbitrary figures have been inserted on a scale from 5 to −5, −5 meaning very hostile, 5 very friendly and 0 neutral. A matrix of this kind has many interesting properties, not all of which can be worked out here but which depend on the kind of restraints that we impose on it. If we suppose, for instance, that the relations of nations are reciprocal, so that I's attitude towards J is the same as J's towards I, the matrix becomes symmetrical about its major diagonal – that is, the lower left-hand triangle is a mirror-image of the upper right-hand triangle.'[1]

Arguments of this kind may contribute to a process of academic research that will ultimately engender theories of greater validity and utility than those offered in the present work, but they are unlikely to be acceptable to British politicians or officials, or to exercise any direct influence on policy, for at least a generation to come. On the other hand those who take decisions are already accustomed to inquire what decisions were previously taken in similar cases and with what results. By itself, as has already been argued earlier, such reliance on mere precedent or analogy can be dangerously misleading. Indeed, it is the whole purpose of this book to argue that the amorphous mass of experience requires to be ordered and disciplined by a skeleton of theory. But, as this theory is specifically intended for the use of practitioners in foreign policy, it can more conveniently be illustrated and supported by reference to the recorded actions of other practitioners than by purely imaginary concepts, whether historical,

[1] K. E. Boulding, essay on 'National Images and International Systems' in *The Theory and Practice of International Relations*, edited by Olson and Sondermann, Englewood Cliffs, N. J. (Prentice Hall 1966).

philosophical or mathematical, particularly when the ultimate validity of these is open to question and their relevance and familiarity are obviously inferior.

It must nevertheless not merely be admitted, but actually emphasized, that the phenomena of international relations are incapable of truly objective perception and that no theory which relies on necessarily subjective analysis of past actions can ever pretend to scientific authority or even, perhaps, to academic respectability. The most that can be said for any theory of foreign policy is that it helps to promote, in those who have studied it, the habit of thinking methodically about the practical problems they encounter. The better the method suggested, the better the results may be, but even a bad method that provokes thought may be preferable to reliance on experience, intuition and judgement, particularly if the thought provoked is so intense as actually to lead to the evolution of a new and superior method. A theory too massive or too unfamiliar may be rejected or ignored: an irritant of the right kind and size can occasionally produce a pearl.

7
OBSTACLES

'Le duopole thermonucléaire et l'extension planétaire du système diplomatique font l'originalité de la conjoncture actuelle. Ces deux faits déterminent la hiérarchie des acteurs et les relations qu'ils entretiennent. Les duopolistes ont une position privilégiée, ils sont seuls à posséder le statut de grande puissance, au sens traditionnel du terme, c'est à dire seuls capables de choisir souverainement entre la guerre et la paix.'

Aron[1]

SOME readers might accord a provisional assent to the arguments of the first five chapters, yet – without endorsing any of the objections considered in the sixth – question the contemporary relevance of this book's central thesis. To them the obstacle might be the apparent inadequacy, in the second half of the twentieth century, of seeking a basis for British foreign policy in the aspirations, interests and capacities of the British people alone. Such readers might have no theoretical objection to nationalism; they might even regard a specifically British foreign policy as desirable; they would merely contend that such a policy could have little practical significance, because the British Government no longer retain any major options in world affairs.

Previous chapters, for instance, have been largely concerned with the factors influencing British governments in 'the identification of disputes with other governments and in the choice of methods for the prevention, limitation and termination of such disputes'. It would thus seem a

[1] Raymond Aron, *Peace and War: A Theory of International Relations*, Chapter 15 (Weidenfeld and Nicolson, London 1966).

formidable obstacle if it could be shown that these processes are either wholly or partially inapplicable to those disputes likely to be of the greatest importance to the British people.

Let us suppose, for instance, that a dispute arises between the Soviet Union and the United States of such gravity and intensity that both governments are prepared to accept the risks of mutual destruction in nuclear war rather than give way, what difference would it make whether or not the British Government identified this as a dispute involving themselves and what significant contribution could the British Government make to the prevention, limitation or termination of such a dispute?

It is easy to imagine circumstances in which the answer to all these questions would be 'none'. An American – or a Russian – leader who had brought himself to the point of accepting the prospect of 'megadeaths' among his own people would scarcely be deterred from pressing the fatal button by anything the British Government could say or do. The destructive capacity under the unfettered control of the United States Government is so great that the additional 'overkill' which might or might not be forthcoming from British nuclear weapons or from American bases in the British Isles (bearing in mind that American missile submarines based on Holy Loch would presumably all put to sea at an early stage of the crisis) would surely not determine the choice between peace and war either in Washington or in Moscow. Nor is it obvious that the British Government would even retain the option of contracting out of the dispute. A declaration of neutrality, even reinforced by the effective and manifest placing under British control of all American bases in the British Isles, might not outweigh in Russian eyes the military advantage of eliminating a potentially hostile country possessing a nuclear strike capability which, if it were to survive the mutual destruction of the Super-Powers, might no longer be insignificant. Is complete certainty possible that, once American leaders were exposed to the actual agonies of thermo-nuclear destruction, even the United States Government would accept with passive resignation the last-minute defection of an ally? Any such war between the United States and the Soviet Union would thus involve at least the risk of intolerable damage to the British nation-state, if not through deliberate attack, then from missiles falling short, from crashing aircraft, from radio-active fall-out or from the destruction or contamination in other countries of the sources of essential British imports. Thermo-nuclear war has not yet been attempted, so its potential repercussions remain incalculable. In spite of all the analyses and predictions of Dr. Kahn and his colleagues, nobody can be sure how these fantastic weapons would function in practice or how rational their controllers would remain once their countrymen had sustained the first few million casualties. But one probability is obvious: accidents are more frequent in war than in peace, because the need to take risks and the tension induced in all concerned lead to a relaxation of safety precautions. Whenever conventional weapons have been employed in war since 1939 major errors have occurred in the targets actually struck by bombs, shells, rockets or even airborne troops. The conflict in Vietnam has demonstrated that the latest refinements of technology have not eliminated such errors from the operations of manned aircraft and the layman may be permitted an equal scepticism concerning ballistic missiles.

The destruction of the British nation-state as an incidental, perhaps even an accidental, consequence of a dispute to which the British Government were not a party and which they were unable to prevent, limit or determine is an appalling but not an impossible conception. In 1962 a dispute arose between the United States and the Soviet Union concerning Cuba. Its origin and the intentions of the contestants are likely long to remain the subject of controversy, but most people would agree that this crisis might, if it had been less cautiously handled, have led to nuclear war and that, in its crucial phase, there was nothing that the British Government could, or did, do to influence its development. Once Russian missile sites had been identified in Cuba, there was a direct confrontation between the United States and the Soviet Union in which neither manifested any inclination to consult other governments before reaching decisions. Nor did the time factor allow much opportunity for the British Government to take an initiative of their own. The first reasonably reliable evidence of a medium-range missile site in Cuba reached Washington on 15 October 1962. There followed five days of unremitting discussion among American leaders of the courses open to the United States Government. Two of those seriously considered were an aerial bombing attack on the missile sites and certain Cuban airfields and an invasion of Cuba. According to Mr. Abel,[1] the final decision to prefer a naval blockade as the first step was reached only on the morning of 21 October. At luncheon that day President Kennedy told the British Ambassador of the decision he had taken. This was the first notification[2] to any ally of the United States of the existence of a major crisis, a distinction probably due to the personal friendship between the Ambassador and the President. By the time the Ambassador's report had been considered by the British Government 156 intercontinental ballistic missiles were ready for firing and bombers of the Strategic Air Command had been ordered into the air with their weapons. By the time the British Prime Minister telephoned President Kennedy to assure him of British support, the President had broadcast his challenge to the

[1] Elie Abel, *The Missiles of October* (MacGibbon & Kee 1966).

[2] Thanks to the alertness of certain British officials in Washington, the Ambassador had been able to send a private warning to the British Government forty-eight hours earlier that a crisis was probably imminent, though the evidence seems to have been too speculative to constitute a basis for any British intervention, had this been desired. (Abel, op. cit.)

Soviet Union, a challenge taken so seriously by the United States Government that, twelve hours later, on the morning of 23 October, the U.S. Secretary of State could remark to one of his subordinates:

> 'We have won a considerable victory. You and I are still alive.'[1]

Certain writers, notably Dr. Kahn, have, in retrospect, tended to minimize the dangers of the Cuban crisis and to argue that this never reached a very high rung on the ladder of escalation towards nuclear war. A different view was taken by those more closely involved at the time. Mr. Macmillan, for instance, later told the House of Commons:

> 'I must say . . . that the week of the Cuban crisis – and I have been through some in peace and war – was the week of most strain I can ever remember in my life. It then seemed to many of us . . . that in the struggle of wills between the Soviet Union and the Western powers, primarily the United States, the world might be coming to the brink of war.'[2]

It is at least arguable that, once President Kennedy had committed the United States Government by his broadcast on the evening of 22 October – a broadcast reinforced, as watchers of British television will remember, by photographs of the lids being opened on American missile silos – the possibility of nuclear war existed to a degree beyond the power of the British Government to determine. Perhaps there was a chance for the British Government to intervene during the preceding forty-eight hours, just possibly some influence might have been exerted by British representations during the six days that preceded the broadcast by Moscow Radio on 28 October of Mr. Khruschev's message that:

> 'The Soviet Government . . . has given a new order to dismantle the arms which you described as offensive and to crate and return them to the Soviet Union.'[3]

[1] Abel, op. cit.
[2] *Hansard*, 17 June 1963.
[3] Abel, op. cit.

It is not altogether inconceivable that, had the Soviet Union been more ready to risk nuclear war, a different British policy might have exerted sufficient influence in Washington to avert this danger by persuading the U.S. Government to make concessions. Nevertheless, it seems rather more likely that the threat of nuclear war – and with it the destruction of Britain – was posed on 15 October 1962, that the British Government knew nothing of its imminence before 19 October, were not fully informed before 21 October, would not thereafter have been able significantly to modify American decisions, and, even if they had wished to make a drastic and dangerous reversal of their entire foreign policy in order to seize the doubtful chance of avoiding disaster, had less than a week in which to consider one of the most momentous and controversial choices ever to confront a British Government.

On the available evidence of the 1962 crisis it seems plausible to conclude that, for a brief period, the future existence of the British nation-state was wholly determined by the interaction of the Governments of the United States and the Soviet Union in a dispute to which the British Government were not a party and which they had no significant opportunity to influence. Nor is it necessary to accept the more horrific fantasies of recent writers of fiction[1] to agree that, on some future occasion, the time – and the options – available to the British Government might be even more limited. It might again be irrelevant and ineffective for the British Government to choose between yielding and fighting: the choice might simply be between a bang with or without a whimper.

This, so far as can be judged, was an actual case. It was also a rare case and one which has been deliberately stated

[1] During the Cuban crisis of 1962 President Kennedy discovered that his instructions had been disregarded on two issues of potentially dangerous relevance: American missiles had not been withdrawn from Turkey and an American reconnaissance aircraft flew over Russian territory during the crisis. (Abel, op. cit.)

in a severely limited form. Admittedly the crucial phase of the Cuban crisis was probably too brief, too acute and, in the eyes of the United States and Soviet governments, too dangerous to leave any significant scope for the effective exercise of British influence. But no such crisis – not even the legendary disturbance on the radar screens – is without deeper and slower growing roots accessible in some degree to British intervention. Even if the origins of the 1962 crisis are limited to Cuba alone, it is possible to indicate occasions on which British decisions may have exercised some influence. For instance, when the United States Government broke off diplomatic relations with Cuba in January 1961, these were maintained by Britain; when the United States proclaimed an embargo on trade with Cuba in February 1962, Britain continued not merely to trade but to extend commercial credits; when the United States Government threatened reprisals against countries trading with Cuba or allowing their ships to visit Cuban ports, the British Government refused to discourage British nationals from either course. Indeed, from the moment of Mr. Castro's accession to power in 1959 and in spite of initial differences concerning the supply of British military equipment to the preceding régime, British governments consistently took the view that neither the existence of the Castro régime nor its internal policies were identifiable as a cause of dispute between Great Britain and Cuba. Minor and incidental disputes did arise during this period, which it was British policy to limit or determine by diplomatic methods, but it is arguable that there was a more fundamental, if more discreetly handled, dispute between Britain and the United States concerning the respective attitudes of their two governments towards Cuba. This dispute was only partly ideological: it also turned on the familiar incompatibility between the interests of investors and those of traders. The seizure of foreign assets in Cuba was far more detrimental to American interests than to British, so that it appeared to the United States Government, but not to the British, worth while to sacrifice their trade in the hope of protecting their investments.

This divergence of interest resulted in the adoption of markedly different policies towards Cuba by the Governments of the United States and of Great Britain and caused successive British governments, in defence of British interests, to urge on the United States Government the advantages of a policy of restraint and toleration towards Cuba. Such representations – and those made by other Allies of the United States – may have had only a limited effect at the time, but they must have helped to modify the climate of official opinion in the United States by providing a constant trickle of views more favourable to the Cuban régime than those reaching Washington from other sources. It is not inconceivable, therefore, that the attitude adopted by successive British governments as a result of their interpretation of the national interest exercised a cumulative pressure on American opinion and played some part in the decision of the United States Government, in October 1962, to reject the more extreme courses open to them and to accept Mr. Khruschev's condition for withdrawing Russian missiles – assurances against an invasion of Cuba.

There is no proof that the views of their allies determined the decision of the United States Government, but it is worth recalling that the Soviet Government apparently put forward two different conditions for the removal of their missiles from Cuba. Mr. Khruschev's letter of 26 October to President Kennedy has not been published, but the President referred to this in his reply of 27 October as proposing only two American concessions: removal of the blockade and assurances against an invasion of Cuba. This interpretation was implicitly confirmed by Mr. Khruschev's reply of 28 October. But there had been another letter from Mr. Khruschev between that of 26 October and the President's reply of 27 October. This other letter – which was actually broadcast by Moscow Radio on 27 October – called for a reciprocal undertaking by the United States Government to remove American missiles from Turkey.[1] This demand – indeed the entire letter of 27 October – was ignored in President Kennedy's reply. Yet according to Abel,[2] the President had himself ordered the removal of these missiles – because they were unreliable, inaccurate and obsolete as well as provocative – well before the crisis began. This order had not been carried out because Turkish objections were expected. In August the President had apparently been prepared to disregard these objections but, in October, he realized that

> 'this was not the time for concessions that could wreck the Western alliance, seeming to confirm the suspicion Charles de Gaulle had planted, that the United States would sacrifice the interests of its allies to protect its own security'.[2]

Instead he preferred to make a concession which, though welcome to the allies of the United States, was repugnant to a substantial section of American opinion and contrary to the policy he himself had previously followed. He agreed to give assurances against an invasion of Cuba, assurances not limited, as had previously been the case, to the armed forces of the United States. Can anyone be certain that President Kennedy and his advisers would have made that choice – and that their successors would have continued to honour the undertaking – if the governments of Britain and of other countries allied to the United States had not earlier made clear their support for measures of collective defence and their opposition to measures intended only to change the ideological character of the Cuban régime? These allies may not have been consulted between 15 and 22 October,

[1] See *The Cuban Crisis of 1962: Selected Documents and Chronology*, edited by David L. Larson, Boston (Houghton Mifflin 1963).

[2] Abel, op. cit.

but it would surely be going too far to contend that the views they had earlier expressed and were known still to hold exercised no significant influence on the anguished deliberations of American leaders during that crucial week.

Decisions, as argued at the outset of this book, are never reached solely on the merits of the particular problem they are intended to resolve. There is always a background of assumptions and preconceptions, a climate of opinion in which reports are assessed and alternatives considered. In the Cuban crisis of 1962 it is possible to distinguish two main currents in the converging streams of history that helped to shape the decisions of President Kennedy and his advisers. There was the long American involvement in the affairs of Cuba and there was the state of tension and hostility existing between the United States and the Soviet Union. Each of these currents had, in earlier years, received some significant influence from British foreign policy. In October 1962 it is unlikely that anyone in Washington recalled that, a century earlier, the United States Government had contemplated war first with Great Britain and later with Spain and France over Cuba or even remembered the benevolent attitude ultimately adopted by the British Government towards American annexation of Cuba in 1898. But these, and the innumerable other Anglo-American exchanges on Cuba, must have modified in some degree the climate of American opinion and may thus have helped to determine American attitudes in the hour of crisis.

So did the extraordinary state of relations between the Soviet Union and the United States in 1962, a situation in which each country believed its survival to depend on the ability instantly to destroy the other. This is such a new and unprecedented phenomenon in the history of the world that some British observers are inclined to regard it as a condition of mutual paranoia attributable only to the national characteristics of the two peoples concerned and to the development of thermo-nuclear weapons. Such critics forget the long absence of significant contact between the two countries, the failure of nuclear capabilities to produce any corresponding tension between Britain and France and the extent of British responsibility for the present state of relations between the Soviet Union and the United States. It is the last factor which is most relevant to the present argument. From 1941 to 1946 successive British governments had to struggle against a consistent American tendency to support Russian interests against those of Great Britain and other countries of Western Europe: the Arctic convoys, strategy in the European campaign, holding 21st Army Group back from Berlin, the evacuation of areas of Germany occupied by British and American forces, O.S.S. aid to Ho Chi Minh, the Yalta Agreement, American hostility to British intervention against the Greek Communists. It would, of course, be misleading to ascribe this tendency to any inherent preference for Russians rather than Britons or even to suppose that the American leaders concerned fully realized what they were doing. There is little evidence to support the theory that the Roosevelt administration consciously contemplated the division of the British Empire and the British sphere of influence between the United States and the Soviet Union. It is not inconceivable, however, that during the immediate post-war period, the Soviet Government may have entertained such an interpretation of American policy and that this may have influenced their selection of British interests as their main target in those years.

Certainly this was a period in which British governments were acutely conscious of the danger to be expected from Soviet power and of the urgency of awakening the apparently complacent Americans to its existence. Doubtless this awakening would have come eventually, but it was probably hastened, perhaps even sharpened, by deliberate British policy. American writers, for instance, habitually emphasize the impact of Sir Winston Churchill's famous 'Iron Curtain' speech at Fulton in 1946, not because its message was then unknown to Americans, but because their Government had hitherto been unwilling themselves to admit, still less, to proclaim its implications. This was a phase which may be said to have ended with the Truman Doctrine of 1947 (itself due to a British initiative) and which might, admittedly, have come to an end soon afterwards without any pressure from British governments or even in spite of pressures in an opposite sense. The final and effective causes of historical events can never be established with certainty and precision, nor can anyone pretend to calculate the permutations of a single variant move in the multi-dimensional chess of international affairs. The most that can tentatively be suggested is that that attitude manifested by President Truman in 1947 was radically different from that of President Roosevelt in 1945 and that one of the factors responsible may have been the influence of British foreign policy during the preceding five years.

This influence was soon to be exerted in a different, sometimes even a contrary, direction. Mr. Attlee's flight to Washington in December 1950, Lord Avon's exertions at Geneva in 1954, Lord Home's in 1961: these – and many others – were instances of British efforts to moderate and restrain the American conviction that only force could contain or frustrate the implacable hostility of the Soviet Union. Once again, no one can pretend to be sure how far British influence was decisive. It is often convenient, when the national interest dictates a course of action difficult to reconcile with national aspirations, to present the choice actually made as a reluctant concession to an importunate ally. Perhaps Mr. Dulles and Admiral Radford never seriously intended American aircraft to intervene in the battle of Dien Bien Phu; perhaps compromises would always have been reached even in the absence of British representations in their favour. What is certain is that, ever since 1940, successive British governments have made great efforts to influence American policy and that the decisions subsequently reached by the Government of the United States, whether these are considered individually or as trends revealing themselves over a period of years, have often approximated to those earlier advocated by the British Government. In particular cases, whether in the past or yet to come, there may be no opportunity for specific British representations or these may be rejected or ignored. But there is sufficient probability that British policy will influence either the particular decisions of the United States Government or else the climate of opinion in which decisions are reached, to give the British Government at least the chance of an option even in those fundamental issues involving the life or death of the British nation-state. And, as long as there is even a chance, that option should be exercised and the factors determining the British Government's choice are still of importance to the British people.

Nevertheless the chance of an option is not a sovereign choice and the very arguments that sustain the continued ability of the British Government to influence most decisions affecting the British people also confirm their potential impotence in those crises which, if they have so far been the rarest, are also the most dangerous and the most liable to prove definitive. Thermo-nuclear missiles have transformed the environment in which British foreign policy operates as the fast motor-car has transformed the conditions of travel by road. In the era of the horse, riders, and drivers could reasonably rely on their own skill and prudence to preserve them from serious accidents. But even the ideal motorist in the perfect car constantly runs the risk of unavoidable death or injury from the folly, recklessness or incompetence of others. He can reduce this risk by his own conduct: he can never eliminate it. To be entirely safe, he must remain indoors: an option not open to British Foreign Secretaries.

It would be dangerous to press this analogy too far, but it does suggest certain questions. Should British governments merely accept the heightened risks, as British motorists have accepted those of the road, and endeavour to minimize them by continued application of the traditional principles of foreign policy? Or ought the avoidance of danger now to be accorded priority over the need to travel? So far it has not. If 'peace' means the avoidance of nuclear destruction, this has not been 'the supreme purpose of all policy'.[1] Some British decisions have obviously served this purpose, whether by restraining the United States Government, by promoting the control of nuclear weapons or by encouraging a better understanding between the Super-Powers. But British motives seldom seem to have been unmixed: moderation is more often preached in Asia than in Europe or the Middle East; British nuclear weapons have not been renounced; there is no disposition to encourage understanding between the United States and the Soviet Union at Britain's expense. And other British decisions have seemed positively to increase the risk of Britain's destruction in nuclear war – the acceptance of U.S. bombers in British bases in 1948 and, subsequently, of other American delivery systems; British participation in the Korean War; British support for the United States in the Cuban crisis of 1962. These decisions may have been rationalized by the argument that any increase in the immediate peril was outweighed by its reduction in the long term, but this argument depends on considerations independent of the mere avoidance of nuclear war. There has always been a multiplicity of objectives: the dangers of the road have never been regarded as an absolute disincentive to travel. Ought they to be? Have the altered dimensions of international relations, the higher power to which their perils have been raised, so transformed the environment in which British foreign policy operates as to require a radical revision of its

[1] See Chapter 2.

basis? If so, is it possible to conceive of a different approach to foreign policy offering a significantly higher probability of avoiding nuclear destruction than anything so far suggested in this book?

Before attempting to consider this difficult and important question, its scope and purpose need to be clarified. A different approach to foreign policy is not the same as a new foreign policy, which might entail nothing more than the adoption of a new doctrine,[1] whereby analysis of the present state of international relations led to an altered line of conduct still ultimately deduced from the same premises. During the sixties, for instance, the working assumptions of British foreign policy might have been expressed in the following doctrine. Great Britain, as a small and densely populated country, is permanently and ineradicably in a position of such disadvantage compared to either of the Super-Powers, that no nuclear strike capacity which could ever be developed from British resources alone would constitute an effective deterrent to the threat of annihilation with which either could confront the British nation-state. Even without invoking economic or political considerations, therefore, it could be argued that Britain must be able to count on the support of one Super-Power if the inherent vulnerability of the British Isles is not to leave them permanently exposed to pressures they could not otherwise resist. If both Super-Powers demanded the same concession from Britain, or if one demanded it while the other remained passive, acquiescence would be the only alternative to annihilation. But protection against such perils is not to be had without a price, for the Super-Power that seeks to deter an attack on Britain thereby increases the risk of an attack on itself. It thus becomes necessary to seek the protection of that Super-Power whose price is most likely to be compatible with British national interests, aspirations and capacities. The choice has fallen on the United States and the price

[1] See Chapter 3.

paid by Britain for American protection has been a general conformity with the policies of the United States and, to a lesser degree, with the policies of other nations under American protection. The working formula for British foreign policy thus becomes to obtain the maximum protection at the minimum price or, in other words, to endeavour to increase the credibility of the American nuclear deterrent in so far as this serves to protect Britain, while simultaneously opposing any tendency towards the use or threat of nuclear warfare in disputes irrelevant to vital British interests.

Given the existence of nuclear duopoly, this working formula for what, in the fashionable jargon of the day, might be called British macro-policy (as distinct from the micro-policy concerned with disputes unlikely ever to involve conflict with or between the Super-Powers) can rationally be deduced from the traditional premises of British foreign policy as these have been earlier expounded in the present work. It is not, however, the only doctrine that could be so deduced. Any fundamental alteration in the present state of affairs, whether in the world as a whole or even inside Britain, might require a new doctrine. Fresh technological developments, more rapid nuclear proliferation, a major political upheaval within either Super-Power or a genuine reconciliation between them might so transform the present nuclear duopoly as to make existing British policy out of date. Even if the rest of the world remained the same, a radical change in the British social order could so alter the requirements of British national interest and aspirations as to cause a fundamental re-alignment of British policy. Yet even a development so dramatic and improbable as a *renversement des alliances* – a substitution of the Soviet Union for the United States as Britain's protector – would not necessarily imply any change in the basic premises of foreign policy. The nature of national interests and aspirations might alter, but not their importance in determining policy.

Even in retrospect it is possible to imagine British governments reacting differently to the international problems of the last two decades. Finland and Sweden, for instance, are in most respects even more vulnerable than Britain to the potential menace of the Soviet Union, yet their governments, while equally concerned with preservation of the nation-state, chose not to seek American protection. Australia and New Zealand, on the other hand, are geographically immune from most forms of pressure from either the Soviet Union or other Communist countries, but have thought it necessary to pay an even higher price than Britain for the shield of American power. France, having once been among the most dependent and committed of the clients of the United States, has since adopted a position of considerable detachment and professes readiness to defend herself against all quarters. Even British governments, while remaining faithful to the basic doctrine, have permitted themselves considerable latitude in its interpretation, sending troops to Korea, but not to Vietnam, supporting the United States over Cuba, but not over Formosa, even briefly and unsuccessfully defying both Super-Powers at once over Suez.

However important and even startling a departure some future British Government might make from the existing doctrine of macro-policy, this would not constitute a new approach as long as it was based on the old premises with their priority for the preservation of the nation-state and their clear distinction between the purpose of Britain and the external environment in which this purpose is pursued. A new approach would have to abandon this duality and to regard foreign policy as being concerned, not with disputes between Britain and foreigners, but with the identification of those problems so crucial to the survival of the human race that only their solution could preserve the British people, an objective which would thus be distinguished from, and accorded a higher priority than, the continued existence of the British nation-state. This is an approach which could easily acquire ethical or ideological overtones, but these are not essential to its justification as long as it is assumed that the survival of the human race is a condition of, rather than an alternative to, the survival of the British people.

There could be more than one such problem – over-population, for instance, is a potential candidate – but it will be sufficient to consider the feasibility of a new approach to foreign policy in terms of the most immediate and obvious threat to human survival: thermo-nuclear warfare. It is difficult to define the extent of this threat with certainty and precision: thermo-nuclear warfare could take so many different forms and its potential consequences extend from the almost negligible to the entirely catastrophic, but one hypothesis is not too improbable to deserve the consideration of the British Government. This is that, in the course of a major nuclear exchange between the Super-Powers and without regard to the balance of advantage between them at the end of the exchange, most of the British people are killed and the British nation-state ceases to exist. This is arguably the worst contingency which any British Government could ever contemplate. Although it can be contended that all men must die sooner or later and may therefore be asked to risk premature death in order to preserve the potentially immortal nation-state, this sacrifice inevitably loses its point if the death of even many millions is likely to prove not only inadequate, but actually irrelevant, to the objective. The independence, the authority, the social order of the nation-state must necessarily be regarded as secondary to its existence and it can scarcely be considered within the competence of a British government to accept any external objective whatsoever as deserving the sacrifice of their own country. If, therefore, it could be shown that the existence of the British nation-state is jeopardized by the pursuit of national interests and aspirations, but that it might be preserved by readiness to sacrifice these objectives in the search for a solution to the problem of nuclear warfare, this would constitute a strong argument for a new approach to foreign policy. *Salus populi suprema lex.* A new approach to foreign policy might also be acceptable, though less attractive, if this could be shown to offer a higher probability of preserving the British people even at the cost of the partial or complete extinction of the nation-state. There is always a chance of restoring a nation-state as long as the people composing it continue to exist and the great majority of Austrians and Czechs probably have cause to be grateful for the acquiescence of their governments, during the late thirties, in what proved to be only a temporary extinction of those nation-states.[1]

So far, it will be observed, these objectives do not extend very far beyond the permissible limits of deduction from our original premises. There are many instances in British history of *either* the independence *or* the authority *or* the social order of the nation-state being partially sacrificed to other objectives and, although it would be unprecedented, it would not be inconceivable for a British government to abandon all three if so desperate a course appeared to offer the only hope of preserving the British people and thus the potential existence of the nation-state. The final rupture with all ideas previously entertained by British governments occurs only when it is suggested that the British people, as well as their nation-state, might have to be sacrificed in order to preserve human civilization in other parts of the world. Lord Russell, for instance, who has long advocated World Government as the only method of avoiding the extinction of 'scientific man', once suggested that this could be achieved by the victory of the Western Powers over the Soviet Union and her allies. He said:

'If there is war, the destruction, especially in our own country,

[1] Written before 21 August 1968.

will probably very greatly exceed what happened in the last war. But I have little doubt that, in the end, the side led by the United States will be victorious. When that happens it is probable that a single military government will be established over the whole world, and that, therefore, great wars will cease . . . mankind may, after the next war, enter upon a period of unexampled peace and prosperity. The future is not all dark: there is a gloomy tunnel to be traversed, but beyond that a gleam of daylight begins to be visible.'[1]

Lord Russell has himself subsequently abandoned this particular variant of his proposition in the light of the new situation created by the increased destructiveness of nuclear weapons and their acquisition in large numbers by the Soviet Union and, although the official American view that 'no one can realistically think of "victory" in a full-scale nuclear exchange',[2] is not universally accepted, it can no longer seriously be contended that such a victory would possess much significance for the British people. Nor is it plausible that war between the Super-Powers could result in a 'single military government . . . over the whole world' after a nuclear exchange so limited as to leave a substantial proportion of the British people with an undiminished expectancy of life. A limited nuclear war terminated by concessions from one of the combatants is quite conceivable, but these concessions would almost certainly be equally limited in character and likely to prove the cause of future and possibly less restricted wars. Any British Government that endeavoured to save the human race by precipitating a nuclear war for the establishment of world government would thus be exposing the British people to risks greater alike in magnitude and in probability than any advantages that could reasonably be expected to ensue.

Indeed, it is tempting to go even further and to argue

[1] Essay in *Horizon* No. 100 of 1948, by Bertrand Russell.

[2] Mr. Dean Rusk, then U.S. Secretary of State in a speech to the U.S. Senate on 12 August 1963.

that the risks of nuclear war to the survival of the British nation-state and the British people are so great that these should never be incurred in any circumstances whatever and that their avoidance should become, in practice, as well as in rhetoric, 'the supreme purpose of all policy'. Unfortunately, as we have already seen, the British Government no longer command a sovereign choice in such matters. As long as nuclear weapons exist in the world in sufficient quantity, the British Isles will be exposed to annihilation, if not by design then as an incidental consequence of the conflict of others. Moreover, Britain's danger is significantly greater than that of most other countries. In the long run Lord Russell may be right in arguing that 'the peril involved in nuclear war is one which affects all mankind and one, therefore, in which the interests of all mankind are at one':[1] in the immediate future either Super-Power could destroy Britain and, if the other remained passive, survive the consequences of British retaliation. The danger may be universal, but, its incidence is unequal and the British Government, in seeking to prevent the nuclear annihilation of the British people, must obtain the co-operation of other governments who believe their own peoples to be less vulnerable. Any alternative approach to foreign policy which relies on the supposed 'harmony of interests' even in so fundamental an issue as the universal desire to avoid nuclear annihilation is necessarily open to the objection that, in major nuclear warfare, a higher proportion of the British people are likely to die sooner. Americans, Chinese, Russians and even New Zealanders can thus rationally contemplate greater risks in pursuit of their national objectives than would be sensible for a British government. Indeed, among those writers of fiction who choose the subject of conditions after a nuclear holocaust, there is a considerable prevalence of opinion that New Zealand can be

[1] Bertrand Russell, *Common Sense and Nuclear Warfare* (Allen & Unwin 1959).

expected to inherit the earth. And writers of fiction, as Mr. Arthur C. Clarke has plausibly demonstrated,[1] have hitherto proved rather more accurate prophets than most of the pundits.

Indeed, if it is admitted that the supreme national interest is the preservation of the nation-state and that this requires, for Britain even more than for most other peoples, the avoidance of nuclear war, strong arguments are needed to support the contention that national interests constitute an inadequate basis for foreign policy in the nuclear age. Let us suppose, for instance, that the avoidance of nuclear annihilation were to be proclaimed as the sole objective of British policy. Is there any course of action which the British Government could follow on the basis of this objective which would be excluded by an assessment of British national interests, aspirations and capacities in the terms earlier suggested in the present work? If so, would this course of action be appreciably more likely to attain the desired objective?

One possible doctrine might be that of pacifism. The British Government might make it a rule to accept every demand received from a foreign government, if there existed any likelihood that refusal would lead to nuclear war. In such circumstances it is not inconceivable that the Soviet Union would demand the removal of American bases from the United Kingdom and British withdrawal from all alliances or engagements potentially hostile to the Soviet Union and it is arguable, though not certain, that the United States would acquiesce. It is also arguable, though again not certain, that the Soviet Government would be content with British neutrality, as they have been content with Swedish, and would not insist on any form of British alignment with their own policies. It is also conceivable that a wholly pacific Britain would be able to maintain a viable economy, as Sweden does, without American assistance or co-operation. But would the

[1] Arthur C. Clarke, *Profiles of the Future* (Gollancz 1962).

existence of this neutral, pacifist Britain significantly decrease the likelihood of nuclear war between the United States and the Soviet Union, a war in which the prevailing wind, even in the absence of any hostile intention on either side, might be enough to kill most of the British people by radio-active fall-out? Would it not, on the contrary, actually increase the probability of such a conflict by depriving the British Government of most of their ability to influence the United States Government, by exacerbating the American sense of insecurity, by inflating Russian self-confidence? There is no certain answer to any of these questions, but it can surely be argued that the danger which such a policy would reduce – that a British Government would deliberately choose nuclear warfare as a means of promoting national interests – is the least likely way in which the survival of the British people could be jeopardized.

These two extremes – the forcible imposition of world government and complete British submissiveness – are courses of action which could not reasonably be deduced from the basis suggested for British foreign policy in this book. Their implausibility as solutions to the nuclear dilemma does not destroy the case for an alternative approach to foreign policy, which does not rest on the adoption, or on the prospects, of any particular course of action. Their very different nature does, however, illustrate the ease with which opposite deductions may be made from a single premise. This is the danger underlying the central, and in some respects attractive, contention that preoccupation with the identification of disputes may actually generate them, whereas concentration on problems tend to favour their solution. To achieve a new approach to foreign policy it would thus be sufficient, at least in the first instance, to create a new attitude among those in authority. Once the solving of human problems had replaced the promotion of particular national interests as the objective, a different style would emerge in the conduct of Britain's international relations and this new and disinterested consistency in British policy would automatically influence the decisions, first, of the British Government and then of other governments as well.

This is an argument apt to irritate practical men, who prefer to consider specific proposals of which they can reasonably hope to predict the results, but it does nevertheless contain an element of substance, which should not be obscured by its resemblance to the doctrine of Christian Scientists concerning health and medical treatment. There are attitudes of mind which, if sufficiently prevalent among those in authority, can do more good or harm than many specific policies or particular decisions. These are the attitudes which make up the climate of opinion in which choices are taken and which constitute that 'large area of common ground which all can take for granted and which does not need to be explained or demonstrated',[1] a common ground composed of assumptions about what exists, what is likely and what is desirable. A significant alteration in any of these assumptions is bound to be reflected in subsequent decisions even without the conscious and deliberate adoption of a new policy or course of action. The flaw in the argument is that the assumptions to be altered do not concern what is desirable – there is little conflict on that score – but what exists and what is likely. Unless, therefore, the new assumptions correspond more closely than the old to what does really exist and what genuinely is likely, any consequential alteration in the character of British policy must necessarily lack a rational foundation.

One of the basic assumptions in this book is that the interests of the British nation-state can be distinguished from those of other nation-states and that the existence of such distinct interests is a potential source of dispute. It does not follow from this assumption that the existence of separate interests will always lead to disputes, still less that

[1] Strang, *The Diplomatic Career*, op. cit.

these disputes must necessarily take the form of violent or dangerous conflict. On the contrary, it has been argued that, the earlier the existence of a dispute is recognized and the more carefully its implications and potential consequences are considered, the greater will be the chance of finding the most economical means of limiting or terminating the dispute. If the assumption of divided interests is wrong or if false deductions are made from it in particular cases, there may, admittedly, be a risk that the expectation of a conflict of interests – and the attitude of caution or suspicion that this expectation will arouse among those in authority – will actually generate a dispute which might have been avoided by an attitude of manifest trust in the good intentions of the other State concerned. But, if this happens, the existence of the dispute is likely to be diagnosed sooner and the choice of measures for resolving it will probably be greater than in the opposite contingency: a dispute arising when this had been considered impossible as a result of a prior assumption of the existence of a harmony of interests. When individual human beings quarrel, it is arguable that the most common cause is simple thoughtlessness: one of them has done something injurious to the interests of another, not because he deliberately intended his interest to prevail over the other's conflicting interest, but simply because it had not occurred to him that the other might have an interest different from his own. If this is also true, as experience suggests is sometimes the case, of nation-states, then the acceptance of a conflict of interests and a readiness to envisage the possibility of disputes should also increase the chances, not merely of limiting or terminating an actual dispute, but even of preventing it from ever starting.

Indeed, one cannot avoid the suspicion that the advocacy of a new approach to foreign policy and of the altered attitudes this would entail is founded, not on any genuine belief in the existence of anything so improbable as the harmony of interests, but on simple distaste for some of the doctrines that have been proclaimed by politicians and theorists who accept the threat of nuclear war as a means of advancing national objectives. Such doctrines, particularly during the fifties and sixties, have found their most striking expression in the United States and the Soviet Union, but even British Foreign Secretaries can, on occasion, turn an arresting phrase. On 3 March 1962, for instance, Lord Home explained to the Northern Divisional Council of the Conservative Association that a cease-fire in Laos had been achieved because the threat of a nuclear conflagration had deterred the Communists. He added, and it is hard to dissent from his view: 'Of course, this sort of policy calls for steady nerves and strong wills.'

He went on: 'Luckily we have an abundant supply of both qualities in these islands.'

It is perhaps understandable that certain implications of these comments should fail to command universal approbation and it might be going too far to argue that all the policies, still less all the public statements, of successive British governments have invariably deserved general applause. But nor could it be argued that these have always been rationally deduced from a correct assessment of national interests, aspirations and capacities. Indeed the contrary view has often been asserted in earlier chapters. But the incorrect application of a principle does not invalidate that principle, unless it can be shown that the principle has an inherent tendency to mislead those who profess it.

This, of course, is the root of the charge against the essentially nationalistic principles suggested as the basis of British foreign policy. On the one hand, it is argued, these create an undesirable duality of outlook: the distinction between the active purpose of Britain and the passive environment – the rest of the world – in which that purpose operates. On the other hand, these principles give rise to a multiplicity of objectives in which effort and imagination are dissipated instead of being concentrated on the single and overriding purpose of avoiding nuclear war.

Duality, however, corresponds to the objective facts. British governments can have no more certainty than individual human beings of correctly or fully comprehending their own purpose, but they are likely to understand it better than the purposes of others. And their purposes, even on so fundamental an issue as nuclear war, are bound to be different. Frequent resort is made by those endeavouring to establish the common purpose of mankind to the analogy of pestilence or natural disaster, but it is an elementary observation that there are always individuals who expect not merely to survive such catastrophies, but actually to profit by them. To assume that all the governments of the world are now convinced, or could speedily be persuaded, that nuclear warfare would deny all nation-states any possibility of advantage would be to disregard both the available evidence and the lessons of history. Therefore, the greater the likelihood that nuclear warfare would indeed be an unmitigated disaster for Britain, the greater the necessity for the British Government to be guided by a rational assessment of their own interests in seeking to prevent it, rather than by the unwarranted assumption that all other governments are equally so concerned.

Similarly, if the policy of the British Government has to be based on the reconciliation of a number of different and often conflicting factors, the mental process of weighing one against another and reaching a balanced conclusion may be productive of delay, compromise and even confusion, but it is more rational and offers a lesser risk of overwhelming error than the subordination of all decisions to a single principle of supposedly overriding and unchallengeable validity. Indeed, it is arguable that the fear of nuclear war that now haunts the imagination of so many has its firmest foundation in just this tendency, in both the Soviet Union and the United States, to subordinate national interests to dogma. It would be difficult to argue that the independence, the authority or the social order of either Super-Power would be enhanced or could only be preserved, by nuclear war against the other. Yet the conflicting dogmas of Communism and anti-Communism appear, at least intermittently and to an appreciable extent, to have persuaded responsible Americans and Russians that there exists an irreconcilable conflict between their two countries. Probably most Americans and most Russians would deny – as both governments have frequently denied – that their own dogma could ever require them to take the initiative in launching a nuclear war: the carefully and expensively maintained capacity of each Super-Power instantly to destroy the other is avowedly defensive. Yet, in each country, the dogma of the other appears so inherently evil and aggresive that attack, by one means or another, is sincerely and constantly feared. Whatever the respective merits of these dogmas, therefore, their influence on the policies of the Super-Powers and on the prospects of world peace can only be regarded as deplorable. They may be contrasted with the addiction of France and Britain to policies based on national interest. Each country possesses nuclear weapons capable of inflicting intolerable damage on the other; there is a long record of mutual war; there have recently been innumerable disputes between the two governments. Yet neither credits the other with aggressive intentions or feels itself threatened by the nuclear armoury of the other. In the absence of dogma there is mutual confidence that reason will prevail.

Nor is it enough to argue that, whereas Communism and anti-Communism are each, in their different ways, irrational, and consequently dangerous dogmas, the principle of the overriding importance of avoiding nuclear war is inherently reasonable and beneficent. There have been many such dogmas in the history of the human race, some of them of apparently unassailable innocence and plausibility, but there is none which has not proved capable of supporting disastrous deductions. No one would impugn Lord Russell's reasoning powers or his good intentions, but there are many millions of people alive today with cause for gratitude that, in 1948, national interests prevailed over his logical deduction from dogma that:

> 'There is one further step which ought to be taken by the United States and Great Britain jointly and that is to inform the Soviet Government . . . that any further breach of treaty will be treated as a *casus belli* . . . in the policy of the Western Powers, there should be two paramount aims. First, to secure peace if possible; second, if that is not possible, to secure victory.'[1]

Lord Russell has subsequently pointed out[2] that

> 'my aim then as now, was to prevent a war in which both sides possessed the power of producing world-wide disaster.'

and has argued, entirely reasonably, that

> 'the policy I have advocated has changed from time to time. It has changed as circumstances have changed. To achieve a single purpose, sane men adapt their policies to the circumstances. Those who do not are insane'.

Unfortunately history suggests that a single purpose is insufficient. Above all, today, in a world where the dimensions and the pace of change are unprecedented, there is no threat to reason more dangerous than the rigidity of mind and the reluctance to adapt and compromise that inevitably flow from the belief that one possesses a single and incontestable revelation of anything so variable and diffuse as truth. The possibilities of error are beyond the ability of man to eliminate, but it is arguable that they can more easily be reduced by requiring proposals to meet

[1] Article in *Horizon* previously quoted.

[2] Bertrand Russell, *Common Sense and Nuclear Warfare*, op. cit., Appendix II.

many criteria than by demanding conformity with only one. What the independence of the nation-state fails to indicate may be supplied by consideration of its authority; the course of action dictated by national interests may be corrected by national aspirations; a faulty assessment of the first and the misguided emotion of the second may still be subdued by the calculation of national capacities. The more governments have to think of, the fewer errors they may commit.

It has not, however, been the purpose of this chapter to consider whether or not British governments have actually erred in the policies they have adopted towards the menace of nuclear war, nor to suggest which courses of action might be best calculated to preserve the British people from the dangers confronting them. We are still concerned with basic principles rather than their detailed application. The question at issue has been whether the destructive capacity of nuclear weapons, and their uneven distribution, have created insuperable obstacles to any British foreign policy based on principles derived from the experience of different eras of human development. Two such obstacles have been considered. The first was that British governments might, in certain circumstances, no longer be able to determine the fate of the British people. The second was that, in seeking to protect the interests of their own people, they might be neglecting the only chance of preserving their existence: concentration on the prevention of nuclear war.

Though both are based on an analysis of the same phenomenon of nuclear duopoly, these are different and, to some extent, incompatible arguments; the first, that the decisions of the British Government are irrelevant and insignificant; the second that these are directed to the wrong objective. There is some force in both arguments. It is true that the British Government may occasionally be unable to exercise an effective choice between life and death for the British people. It is also true that, by comparison with the urgency of Britain's need to avoid a nuclear war, all her other interests and aspirations are the idle fancies of a parish councillor. But, so it is here asserted, the want of omnipotence is no reason for abstention from such choices as are available, nor can the predominant danger more effectually be averted by the neglect of others. In the great game of international relations the stakes have been immeasurably increased, the range of possible gambits has been reduced, but the basic rules are unchanged. It only remains to apply them correctly.

8

THE GENERAL CONCEPTION

'The main danger of theory lies in its abstract nature. The foreign policy of every single state is an integral part of its peculiar system of government. Hence generalizations embracing all States tend to lose sight of the political realities they are studying."

Frankel[1]

THE Manual of Infantry Training used to include, as its only epigram, the reflection that time spent in reconnaissance was seldom wasted and this protracted exploration of means and motives has been directed to a definite end: the interests, the aspirations and the capacities of Britain have been analysed as components of a general conception of British foreign policy and as criteria for testing the validity either of actual policies or of those which might in future be elaborated to replace them. No electrician, for instance, could appraise or assemble a circuit without a similar knowledge of the properties and values of the resistances, the capacities and the inductances it must necessarily contain. But he must also have some more general idea of the nature of the circuit which is to unite these factors and to make them serve a specific purpose. It should already be obvious that any general conception of British foreign policy needs to satisfy a number of particular requirements: what remains to be established is the nature, purpose and characteristics of the unifying framework. Once we have put the individual questions – what does Britain want, what does she need, of what is she

[1] Joseph Frankel, *The Making of Foreign Policy*, Preface (Oxford University Press 1963).

capable? – how do we frame the resultant query; has the purpose of Britain been usefully stated?

It will scarcely have escaped the attentive reader that most of the questions suggested in earlier chapters admit of more than one answer. The components of policy are so various, so potentially conflicting, so little susceptible of indisputably objective perception, that even similar methods of analysis must necessarily lead different men to diverse conclusions. However earnestly we endeavour to pin down the true nature of the national interest, to match it with only the most relevant and obvious of national aspirations and to weigh both against a clinically detached assessment of national capacities, it would be idle to pretend that only one general conception could rationally emerge. Even if this process could be undertaken by beings both infallible and omniscient the result of their calculations would still be ephemeral. Every component of policy is subject to a process of change as continuous as it is often unpredictable. The authority of the nation-state did not possess the same practical significance or the same relative value in 1968 as it did in 1938. Nor is it only the power and purpose of Britain that alter: so does the international environment in which these operate.

This environment has received only incidental consideration in this book, for it constitutes a separate subject, vaster, far more complex and even more variable. It deserves – and it has received – many treatises in its own right. Yet it is indissoluble from any conception of British foreign policy, which necessarily depends on assumptions about the nature of the world and the intentions and abilities of its alien inhabitants. Maintenance of the social order, for instance, has been suggested as one of the motive forces of British foreign policy, but the nature of its influence could as easily be transformed by foreign as by domestic revolutions. Its relevance would not exist unless it were dependent on foreign co-operation or menaced by foreign hostility. Indeed, the assessment of every British objective is so intimately affected by likely foreign reactions that many writers have preferred an altogether different approach; they have started with a systematic presentation of the international scene and only thereafter have sought a rôle for Britain to play on the stage they have first set for her.

Nor is it only writers who are thus addicted to amateur dramatics: statesmen at home and abroad are for ever expatiating on Britain's rôle – or lack of one. This is understandable – drama is an essential element of politics – but it has serious theoretical weaknesses. It is difficult enough to understand and to reduce to a coherent system the complexity of British means and motives, but the task of deriving these from a theory embracing the entire human race is necessarily subject to a far greater factor of uncertainty and error. Moreover, it conflicts with the basic assumptions of the present work: that the British people exist; that they have ascertainable needs and desires; and that the purpose of British governments is to satisfy these needs and desires to the extent that British capacities permit. The views of foreigners are directly relevant to the capacities of the British people, but it would surely be going too far to suggest that these should determine what the British people require or want. There is some sense in that other military precept that any appreciation must begin by a statement of the objective and only thereafter consider the obstacles or the resources that might influence its attainment. It is an ordinary observation of everyday life that success more often rewards those who select and pursue specific objectives than those whose conduct is determined solely by the desire to placate the often conflicting and imperfectly understood aspirations of others. 'What is there in it for us?' may seem an inelegant question, but it is surely a proper test for the British people to apply to any statement of British foreign policy.

Unfortunately it is a question which requires some

elaboration if it is to evoke usefully informative answers. A statement of British foreign policy – and none will be attempted in this book, which is intended only to encourage, and perhaps to assist, its readers in that endeavour – need not be comprehensive and cannot be definitive. The purpose and power of Britain are variable factors in a constantly changing environment. The basic criteria of foreign policy may be reasonably stable, but their practical values and their interaction require as frequent reassessment as does the international situation. The most that can be hoped for is a general doctrine – or an assortment of particular but compatible doctrines – valid only for a given period and set of circumstances whether domestic or foreign. It is nevertheless possible to indicate certain tests which such doctrines ought to pass.

To begin with, no doctrine is useful unless it assists in the making of choices. This is as important to the Foreign Secretary who may have to make up his mind in a matter of hours as it is to the ordinary elector, who cannot be consulted in the moment of crisis. Both need to know in advance what kind of response the British Government will regard as preferable to the kind of problems that can reasonably be foreseen as falling within the scope of the doctrine. This does not mean that the doctrine infallibly indicates the action to be taken – circumstances can alter cases – but that it creates a predisposition towards a particular choice of objective and of means. When, in the small hours of 21 August 1968, the Soviet Ambassador informed the Minister of State at the Foreign Office that Russian troops were entering Czechoslovakia, the prevailing doctrine may not have indicated in precise detail the nature of the British response, but it clearly excluded the two extremes of congratulation or an immediate declaration of war. Indeed it must have limited to a fairly narrow range of choices whatever alternative proposals were submitted to the Foreign Secretary by his officials. This is the first requisite of any useful doctrine: to assist in the identification of disputes and in the choice of methods for their resolution; to indicate which problems matter to the British Government and what categories of British response ought to be considered.

The choice suggested ought naturally to be correct as well as clear. This is more difficult to achieve, but the next test offers some assistance: does the doctrine rest on a prediction that the indicated course of action will have specific results? This may seem an absurdly obvious question, but failure to ask it – or to abide by the answer – has been a frequent cause of misfortune. British governments, for instance, have often conceived it their duty to pass public comment on events abroad: to censure the actions of foreigners, to express sympathy for one side in a dispute between third parties, to recommend to others particular courses of action. Such statements often appear to be made without regard to their probable consequences, the argument being that British governments not only have a right to proclaim their views but are actually under an ethical or ideological obligation to do so. The action is taken for its own sake and not in the expectation of any specific result and when the outcome proves to be the destruction of British Embassies abroad, the molestation of British subjects, the loss of British trade or a run on the pound, the British Government are aggrieved. Such steps are often justified by resort to principles of the kind discussed in Chapter 6. There is no need to recapitulate earlier arguments against their philosophical validity: it is enough to recall that ancient maxim of English law, whereby reasonable men are presumed to desire the natural consequences of their actions and, if these are predictably bad, cannot plead the excuse of good intentions or generous impulses.

If a doctrine indicates a choice and predicts a result, the next step is to ask whether the outcome will be advantageous, whether it is more likely to satisfy, to the extent permitted by national capacities, the aspirations and interests of Britain than would be the predictable result of other policies. Here it is naturally necessary to distinguish between neglect to count the consequences and the deliberate acceptance of immediate disadvantage in the rational expectation of ultimate gain. British membership of the North Atlantic Treaty Organization, for instance, imposes a considerable economic burden which may not be balanced by any immediately tangible rewards. But the doctrine requiring Britain to choose this course rather than that of neutrality rests on a prediction that this will deter a Soviet attack on Britain, prevent a war in Europe and avoid the loss, through the effects of forcible Communization, of valuable trading partners, whereas British withdrawal would make all these disagreeable contingencies more likely. The accuracy of this prediction need not concern us: what matters is that the choice indicated by the doctrine rests on a comparison, which can be tested by reference to national interests and aspirations, of the balance of loss or gain to Britain.

Some doctrines, however, endeavour to balance intangible advantage against material loss. The abstractions most commonly involved are the honour, the prestige, the good name or the rôle of Britain. In 1941, for instance, Churchill considered it preferable to send British troops to certain defeat in Greece (G.H.Q. Cairo started preparing the withdrawal before the first contingents had even landed) rather than to incur the odium of standing idly by while another of Germany's victims met a fate which Britain was in any case unable to avert. His idea that foreigners can be usefully impressed by the quality of British failures is one which dies hard. Even today it is essential to emphasize that prestige is a reputation for success, not a tribute to good intentions. As for Britain's 'rôle', the very word should be enough to discredit any doctrine that employs it. A rôle is the part assumed by an actor to impress an audience, a pretence at characteristics he does not possess. If a given policy can be expected to achieve its stated purpose, it does not need to be justified by its ability to evoke foreign approval, though success will often command an admiration the sincerer for its silence. But the applause which greets a declaration, the striking of a posture, the assumption of a rôle can be prolonged only by evidence that Britain has both an objective and a reasonable expectation of its attainment. No international reputation can be more advantageous to a British Government than that of knowing what they want and how to get it.

How to get it ought to be, but often is not, the most difficult question. It involves an assessment, not only of British capacities, but also of the intentions and abilities of foreign governments. It would be idle to pretend that theory could offer any infallible guide in this perplexing arena, though a number of detailed suggestions have been advanced in earlier chapters, particularly in relation to national capacities. All that can usefully be added here is that a doctrine prescribing particular courses of action as likely to have advantageous results for Britain must necessarily include a prediction of the probable responses of those foreign governments obviously involved. This is a field in which even the experts have notoriously proved to be fallible, but it may nevertheless be possible to suggest certain precepts as tending to eliminate some of the errors to which British governments are particularly susceptible. The first is that the intentions and abilities of foreigners are constantly in evolution; what seemed plausible in 1958 may no longer be so in 1968. The second is that, whereas the intentions of foreigners are commonly more adverse than the British Government suppose, their capacities are usually less. The third is that the resolution, the virtue, the vigour and the power of the British Government are always more highly estimated in London than in any other capital whatsoever.

In the light of earlier arguments we may therefore conclude that a valid general conception of British foreign policy must indicate a choice between different courses of action, must predict the results of the preferred choice, must show this to be to Britain's advantage and must support this prediction by a plausible assessment of foreign reactions as well as of British capacity.

9
APPLICATION

'Those experienced in work must take up the study of theory and must read seriously; only then will they be able to systematize and synthesize their experience and raise it to the level of theory, only then will they not mistake their partial experience for universal truth and not commit empiricist errors.'

'If we have a correct theory, but merely prate about it, pigeon-hole it and do not put into practice, then that theory, however good, is of no significance.'

Mao Tse-Tung[1]

ANY theory of foreign policy can only be tested – it would be absurd to speak of 'proof' – if it is applied over a period of years. It is accordingly necessary, if this book is to serve its avowedly practical purpose, to indicate the kind of choices which the application of this theory would require, to predict their results, to assess their advantages and to estimate their possibility.

One major reservation is needed at the outset. No theory can ever constitute a magic formula. Even if this book contains more truth than error, even if it were one day to be read by a Foreign Secretary, even if he were to believe what he read, there would be no miraculous transformation of foreign policy, no sudden crop of achievements that had eluded his equally conscientious but less fortunate predecessors. The problems posed by foreign policy are not so easily solved, nor can this or any other book pretend to offer an infallible guide across their com-

[1] *The Thoughts of Chairman Mao Tse-Tung.*

plexities. The very most that can be claimed is that this book, or a better one of the same kind, might increase the relevance and precision of the theoretical tools available to the practitioners of foreign policy.

This reservation is not merely prompted by what Mr. Dubcek called 'the dark and real power of international factors . . . the real objectively existing and limiting factor of the possible pace and form of our own political development'.[1] British foreign policy is necessarily restricted by the external environment: the theoretical tools suggested in this book may improve British navigation between Scylla and Charybdis, but cannot abolish those obstacles. Nor, as many thousands of maritime collisions have demonstrated of radar, can they safely be employed without preliminary study and even training. The choice required of a British government that wished to apply this theory would thus be more than intellectual: it would also imply a readiness to make changes of an organizational and educational character. The mere conversion of a Foreign Secretary would be insufficient.

In the twentieth century the nature and conduct of British foreign policy no longer reflect the preferences of an individual leader but those of an organization and an establishment. The way people think about foreign policy, the kind of options they consider, the type of argument they employ: all these are dependent on an intellectual environment which can only gradually be altered. The age has long passed in which the mere advent to office of Lord Palmerston could transform policy, or in which he could claim to be the only man still outside an asylum who had once understood the Schleswig–Holstein question. *L'extension planétaire du système diplomatique* has presented British Foreign Secretaries with more problems than one man could ever hope to master, while the growth of democracy and of mass-communications has increased

[1] Speech by Mr. Dubcek to the Czechoslovak Communist Party Central Committee on 31 August 1968 as reported in *The Times* of 2 September.

the numbers of those able and eager to influence his decisions. Seldom, if ever, can he personally read all the documents bearing on a single problem, make his own analysis, devise his individual solution, put it into effect without reference to his Ministerial colleagues or, above all, complete these complex processes without the distraction and potential embarrassment of public debate. His freedom of action is doubly circumscribed: pressure of business and shortage of time compel him to consider most problems only as these are presented to him by his officials, yet his decisions, often limited to the options already presented to him, must also take account of a political and public opinion shaped by the independent and often incompatible analyses offered by parliament, Press and television, each with their retinue of autonomous and sometime self-appointed experts. His own intellect, his own knowledge, his own assumptions and preconceptions cannot operate in complete independence either of those which pre-digest his problems or of those which judge his solutions.

There is an elementary mathematical conundrum, for instance, of which the perplexity exists only in the manner of its presentation. Three men went out to dinner – this was long ago – and the bill came to 25 shillings. Each gave the waiter a 10 shilling note and, when he brought the change, each pocketed a shilling from the plate, leaving two shillings as the waiter's tip. Each had thus contributed 10 shillings minus 1 shilling, making 9 shillings each or a total of 27 shillings. The waiter received 2 shillings, making a grand total of 29 shillings. So what happened to the other shilling out of the 30 originally laid on the plate or why did whichever British Foreign Secretary make the wrong decision in whichever instance you care to quote?

This is a difficulty experienced by all men handling complex phenomena through a large organization and under the critical and potentially crucial gaze of many interested observers. Although the complexities are greater, the pace faster and the stakes higher, it is essentially the same difficulty that confronts the managing director of some great commercial enterprise, who must simultaneously rely on his staff and satisfy his board and shareholders. It is a matter of management and good management is increasingly recognized as now demanding more than individual flair, judgement or brilliance. The problems must be properly presented from below and the solutions must be readily comprehensible above. There must also be a common language, a similar background of assumptions and theoretical concepts. The best of executives will find his own mastery of discounted cash flow or critical path analysis useless if his subordinates cannot handle these tools or his directors cannot understand the results.

The rule-of-thumb derived from the interpretation of experience in the light of a general education is increasingly being recognized as inadequate for the management of large commercial enterprises. Special skills, new techniques and specific training are now demanded by the largest and most successful firms. In June 1968 the Fulton Committee extended this idea to the British Civil Service.

> 'It must be accepted that for the administrator to be expert in running the government machine is not in itself enough. He must in future also have or acquire the basic concepts and knowledge . . . he must have a real understanding of, and familiarity with, the principles.'[1]

This is a dictum which has not hitherto been applied to the practitioners of British foreign policy, be they politicians, officials, journalists, television commentators or even academics. As Lord Strang wrote:

> 'There is really no mystery about diplomacy . . . a Foreign Service Officer . . . learns his craft chiefly by exercising it under the guidance and supervision of the senior officers to whom he is immediately responsible. . . . there is in fact only one qualification

[1] Command 3638 of June 1968, para. 41. H.M.S.O.

required of candidates for the Foreign Service which is not required of those for the Home Civil Service and that is to pass a foreign language test.'[1]

And even the ability to obtain second-class honours in classics or molecular biology followed by interviews and a foreign-language test is not demanded of Foreign Secretaries or of those hundreds or sometimes thousands of other persons who are, from time to time, able to exert a decisive influence on British foreign policy. If the qualifications of the experts are sometimes inadequate or irrelevant, those of others are often non-existent. This absence of qualifications may be inevitable, even desirable, at the very top. In a democracy we, the people, must be allowed the privilege of choosing our leaders for other qualities than expertise. But those who claim a special ability to advise our leaders ought actually to possess it. As Mr. McNamara, no mean expert in these matters, has pointed out:

> 'Vital decision-making, particularly in policy matters, must remain at the top. This is partly, though not completely, what the top is for. But rational decision-making depends on having a full range of rational options from which to choose, and successful management organizes the enterprise so that process can best take place.'[2]

Mr. McNamara goes on to argue that the absence of this kind of management in Europe constitutes the main reason for the so-called technological gap between Europe and the United States and he attributes its absence to European weakness in education, particularly in managerial education. This is not a novel view, but one which has repeatedly been emphasized by the succession of committees and commissions, British and foreign, that have investigated the deficiencies of Britain's economic

[1] Strang, *The Diplomatic Career*, op. cit.

[2] Robert S. McNamara, *The Essence of Security* (Hodder & Stoughton 1968).

organization. It is a view no less applicable to the management of Britain's foreign policy.

This kind of management must naturally be distinguished from pure diplomacy – the art of negotiation. The evolution of foreign policy, its modification in the light of changing circumstances and its translation into specific decisions or instructions requires different qualifications. Lord Strang said that it was:

> 'the quality of judgement which in the Foreign Service is prized above almost all others'.[1]

And it is this quality which must constantly be exercised by those who identify a problem, analyse its significance, present it to the Foreign Secretary and make recommendations for its solution. The same quality is required of everyone else who seeks to influence his decisions. Must this quality be inborn, can it only be developed by trial and error?

Presumably this is not even the official view, or candidates for the Diplomatic Service would not be required to reach certain minimum standards of general education. But, if any education tends to favour the development of judgement, to increase the latent capacity for identifying international disputes and choosing methods for their resolution, would not a specialized, professional education be even more efficacious?

This is a question which need not stand or fall on the merits of this book alone. It has here been contended that the management of foreign policy can be facilitated by the use of specific theoretical concepts and by the application of particular theoretical tests. The validity of each of these concepts and tests is open to argument; it is even conceivable that all of them could successfully be disputed. But there is a great difference between demolishing a particular theory and denying the need for any theory or system at all. Anyone even remotely familiar with the medical

[1] Strang, op. cit.

profession will be aware that doctors seldom agree and the perceptive patient with an intractable complaint can soon assemble his own anthology of discreet dissent: 'perhaps we might try a less daring treatment' or 'yes, indeed, I always used to prescribe that myself before the war'. Nor are these the differences only of individuals: the theory and practice of medicine have always existed in a state of acutely controversial flux where few doctrines command universal acceptance or can long survive the torrent of innovation and experiment. Yet the disputes of doctors and the progress of medicine benefit from being conducted in a common language, on shared assumptions and on the basis of broadly similar systems of professional training. If they agreed on nothing else, the majority of doctors would probably admit that their training had given most of them greater powers of diagnosis, of treatment and of prognosis than could be expected of even unusually brilliant and cultured laymen. It is the contention of this book that an analogous system of professional education would increase the powers of right judgement of the practitioners of foreign policy.

Such an education could take many different forms, particularly in its earlier stages, and elaborate proposals would be inappropriate to the concluding pages of a more restricted thesis. The relative advantages of literacy and numeracy, of economics or of history, need not be debated here. But some instruction in the principles of foreign policy, some study of the theoretical tools employed by its practitioners seems essential. This book may be nonsense, but the student who had dissected it under the guidance of a clever don, who had compared its arguments with those of different authors, who had analysed its historical references and himself dug out others, such a student would surely be better equipped to make judgements on foreign policy than any classicist or mathematician of equal native ability. And these traditional methods of instruction could be supplemented by all the latest devices; the use of scenarios, simulated decision-making, exercises in analysis and in the presentation of options.

To begin with, there might be established – perhaps at one of those Scottish universities where the native respect for education has always exceeded that of the English – a post-graduate Institute of Foreign Policy. There might go, at government expense, the young graduates already selected as otherwise qualified for the Diplomatic Service together with some of the younger and still impressionable serving officers. There they should also encounter, as fellow-students, men and women desirous of acquiring additional qualifications for a career in politics, in journalism or in scholarship. There, too, should be held refresher courses and seminars for those already actively engaged, or merely acutely interested, in the conduct or criticism of foreign policy. There, above all, should be assembled, to teach and to study, the scholars and experts whose wisdom and knowledge should lay the true foundations for a more authoritative and exhaustive theory of foreign policy.

If such an institute were to acquire reputation and authority, it could not only hope to produce an increasing flow of qualified alumni to take their places among the ranks of those who help to decide the destiny of our nation. It would also begin to establish a common language for the public discussion of controversial issues, to encourage the production of books, of articles, of lectures and comments, that would help to educate us all. Thinking, the production of ideas, their modification in the light of events, their dissemination in comprehensible form: these are exacting and time-consuming activities. They should not be expected of those confronted in their daily lives by an incessant flood of telegrams requiring instant decision, by deadlines and division bells, by the need for immediate and televised profundity. There will always be a need for practical men capable of the rapid digestion of problems and the enunciation of swift decisions. But these men are guided, must be guided, even unconsciously, by precepts, by assumptions, by preconceptions formulated by others. The basic criterion of civilization, and its indispensable condition, has always been the ability of society to allow some of its members to sit and think about the nature of the problems that practical men have always had to solve without any personal opportunity for protracted or profound reflection. Somewhere, however distant, however deeply buried, there lurks behind every decision the shadow of the forgotten scholar who first pondered in the seclusion of his encumbered study the abstract principles involved.

As the years passed, it would gradually become the exception, rather than the rule, for foreign policy to be created, conducted or criticized by persons without theoretical knowledge or professional training. The results might not be immediate or spectacular, but it seems reasonable to expect the same gradual improvement in the general level of competence and success as has attended similar reforms in medicine, the law, engineering and other skilled professions. Indeed, the case for this particular change rests on a proposition so elementary as to be almost irrefutable: where one man decides everything, the quality of his decisions will depend on his intellectual and moral capacities rather than on his training, but where many people are involved in the rapid reaching of numerous choices, it is more useful, and easier to arrange, that all of them should possess a common language and a basic store of similar knowledge, than that each of them should have brilliant native talent and individually acquired relevant experience.

The advantages to the British people of increased competence in the management of foreign policy scarcely require argument: never before has their existence – and the still exceptional amenities it offers – been so dependent at every point on the conduct of British relations with foreign States. There may be more appealing, more popular, more exciting avenues for improvement, but efficient foreign relations are as fundamental and as essential to the survival of civilization in Britain as are efficient sewers. And sewerage engineering is no longer a task for the untrained amateur.

As for the possibility of such improvement, there are really only two obstacles: the ingrained English distrust of education and expertise; and the suspicion that demanding qualifications for the conduct of foreign policy will disfranchise those without them. Neither is insuperable, even if the slow, reluctant, partial, glacier-like yielding of the first scarcely encourages excessive optimism about the second. Yet it is an unfounded suspicion. Democratic control of foreign policy is exerted by the expression, through the small minority of those who give voice to mass-opinions, of national aspirations. These aspirations are more likely to be heeded if they are relevant and if those who utter and those who hear them possess a common language. They are more likely to be effective if those who act on them have been trained in the relation of ends to means. The increasing professionalism of the British Army has not diminished the effectiveness of civilian control over its objectives: a trained and educated soldier is not less loyal or disciplined.

Analogies seldom convince the obstinate and there comes a moment when argument must yield to conviction and to the inescapably obvious trend of events. Education and professionalism are gradually infiltrating the British social structure. The end of amateurism is ultimately as inevitable in Westminster and in Whitehall as it is in the City of London. What matters is whether it comes in time to preserve for the British people the unique advantages which the independence, the authority and the social order of their nation-state have conferred on them. These are small islands, their natural resources are sparse and the privileged existence of their inhabitants is no longer supported by any corresponding preponderance of power or monopoly of technological achievement. If the life of the nation is to be agreeably prolonged, the management of its affairs will require systematic thought and trained skill. If this book in any way hastens their application to the conduct of foreign policy its errors will find sufficient excuse and its importunity justification enough.

A SELECTIVE BIBLIOGRAPHY

Anyone interested by the present book will probably find those listed below rewarding. These do not make up a complete list of relevant works, for which an entire volume would be needed. It is not even a list of the best books on each subject. Those included have been chosen for their ability to provoke further thought and purely historical works have not always been included even when these have been cited in the text. Admirable historical bibliographies may, however, be found in the works of A. J. P. Taylor, particularly his *The Struggle for Mastery in Europe 1848–1918*.

In the idiosyncratic list that follows omission does not imply disregard, nor does inclusion entail acceptance of all the ideas expressed.

FUNDAMENTAL

DESCARTES, René – *Discours de la Méthode*, numerous editions since the seventeenth century.

La ROCHEFOUCAULD, François VI Duc de – *Maximes*, Cambridge University Press, Cambridge and New York 1945.

MACHIAVELLI, Niccolo – *The Prince* (English trans. George Bull), Penguin Books, Harmondsworth, Middlesex and Baltimore, Maryland 1961.

VOLTAIRE – *Candide ou l'Optimisme*, numerous editions since 1759.

THEORY OF INTERNATIONAL RELATIONS

The indispensable works on this subject are those of E. H. Carr. Several of those listed below contain extensive bibliographies.

ARON, Raymond – *Peace and War: A Theory of International Relations*, Weidenfeld & Nicolson, London and Doubleday, New York 1966.

BURTON, J. W. – *International Relations: A General Theory*, Cambridge University Press, Cambridge and New York 1965.
CALVOCORESSI, P. – *World Order and New States*, Chatto & Windus, London and Praeger, New York 1962.
CARR, Edward Hallett – *The Twenty Years Crisis*, Macmillan, London and New York 1940; *Conditions of Peace*, Macmillan, London and New York 1942.
FRANKEL, Joseph – *The Making of Foreign Policy*, Oxford University Press, London and New York 1963.
QUANDT, Richard E. – 'On The Use of Game Models in Theories of International Relations', essay in *The International System*, ed. Knorr and Verba, Princeton University Press, Princeton, New Jersey and Oxford University Press, London 1961.

BRITISH FOREIGN POLICY

This section excludes purely historical works.

BISHOP, Donald G. – *The Administration of British Foreign Relations*, Syracuse University Press, Syracuse, New York 1961.
KIRKPATRICK, Sir Ivone – *The Inner Circle* (Chapter X), Macmillan, London and New York 1959.
STRANG, Lord – *The Foreign Office*, Allen & Unwin, London and Oxford University Press, New York 1955; *The Diplomatic Career*, André Deutsch, London 1962.
TAYLOR, A. J. P. – *The Trouble Makers*, Hamish Hamilton, London and Indiana University Press, Bloomington, Indiana 1957.

HISTORICAL

CHURCHILL, Winston – *The Gathering Storm*, Cassell, London and Houghton Mifflin, Boston 1948.
EDEN, Anthony – *Full Circle*, Cassell, London and Houghton Mifflin, Boston 1960.
GRENFELL, Russell – *Main Fleet to Singapore*, Faber & Faber, London and Macmillan, New York 1951.
GREY of Fallodon, Lord – *Twenty Five Years*, Hodder & Stoughton, London and Frederick A. Stokes, New York 1925.
NICOLSON, Harold – *Lord Carnock*, Constable, London and

Houghton Mifflin, Boston 1930; *Peacemaking 1919*, Constable, London and Houghton Mifflin, Boston 1944; *Curzon: The Last Phase*, Constable, London and Houghton Mifflin, Boston 1937; *Diaries and Letters 1930–1939*, Collins, London and Atheneum, New York 1966.

PANIKKAR, K. M. – *Asia and Western Dominance*, Allen & Unwin, London and John Day, New York 1953.

PRESTON, A. and MAJOR, J. – *Send a Gunboat*, Longmans, Green, London 1967.

SETON-WATSON, Hugh – *Neither War nor Peace*, Methuen, London and Praeger, New York 1960.

STRACHEY, John – *The End of Empire*, Gollancz, London and Random House, New York 1959.

STRANG, Lord – *Britain in World Affairs*, Faber & Faber, London and Praeger, New York 1961.

TAYLOR, A. J. P. – *Europe: Grandeur and Decline*, essays on the Traditions of British Foreign Policy and Democracy and Diplomacy – Penguin Books, Harmondsworth, Middlesex and Baltimore, Maryland 1967; *The Origins of the Second World War*, Hamish Hamilton, London and Atheneum, New York 1961; *The Struggle for Mastery in Europe 1848–1918*, Oxford University Press, London and Harcourt, Brace, New York 1957.

THOMAS, Hugh – *The Suez Affair*, Weidenfeld & Nicolson, London and Harper & Row, New York 1966.

WHEELER-BENNETT, John W. – *Munich: Prologue to Tragedy*, Macmillan, London and Duell, Sloan & Pearce, New York 1948.

WOODHOUSE, C. M. – *British Foreign Policy Since The Second World War*, Hutchinson, London and Praeger, New York 1961.

YOUNG, G. M. – *Stanley Baldwin*, Rupert Hart-Davis, London 1952.

STRATEGIC THEORY

HALPERIN, Morton H. – *Limited War in the Nuclear Age*, John Wiley, New York and London 1963.

KAHN, Herman – *On Thermonuclear War*, Princeton University Press, Princeton, New Jersey and Oxford University Press, London 1960; *Thinking About the Unthinkable*, Horizon Press,

New York and Weidenfeld & Nicolson, London 1962; *On Escalation*, Praeger, New York and Pall Mall Press, London 1965.

KISSINGER, H. A. – *Nuclear Weapons and Foreign Policy*, Harper & Row, New York, for the Council on Foreign Relations, and Oxford University Press, London 1957.

SNYDER, William P. – *The Politics of British Defence Policy 1959–1962*, Ohio State University Press, Columbus, Ohio and Ernest Benn, London 1964.

ECONOMIC FACTORS IN FOREIGN POLICY

HARROD, R. F. – *The Life of John Maynard Keynes*, Macmillan, London and Harcourt, Brace, New York 1951.

HOFFMAN, Ross J. S. – *Great Britain and the German Trade Rivalry 1875–1919*, Russell & Russell, New York 1964.

HOSKINS, H. L. – *British Routes in India*, Frank Cass, London and Octagon Books, New York 1966.

KEMP, Tom – *Theories of Imperialism*, Dennis Dobson, London 1967.

KEYNES, J. M. – *The Economic Consequences of the Peace*, Macmillan, London and Harcourt, Brace, New York 1920; *The Economic Consequences of Mr. Churchill*, Hogarth Press, London and Harcourt, Brace, New York 1925; '*Dr. Melchoir*', in *Two Memoirs*, Rupert Hart-Davis, London and A. M. Kelley, New York 1949.

NICOLSON, Harold – *King George V*, Chapters 24, 26 and 27, Constable, London 1952.

PARKINSON, C. N. – *Trade in the Eastern Seas*, Frank Cass, London and A. M. Kelley, New York 1966.

SHONFIELD, Andrew – *British Economic Policy Since the War*, Penguin Books, Harmondsworth, Middlesex and Baltimore, Maryland 1958.

STRACHEY, John – *The End of Empire*, Gollancz, London and Praeger, New York 1959.

STRANG, Lord – *Home and Abroad* (Chapter III), André Deutsch, London 1956.

WAGNER, Richard – *Götterdämmerung*, Act III, Scene III. Sung by Kirsten Flagstad, H.M.V. HQM 1057.

INDEX

The theoretical concepts with which this book is principally concerned are indicated in capital letters — FORCE.

INDEX

INDEX